Clean Your Clothes
With Cheez Whiz®

Other Books by Joey Green

Hellbent on Insanity

The Unofficial Gilligan's Island Handbook

The Get Smart Handbook

The Partridge Family Album

Polish Your Furniture with Panty Hose

Paint Your House with Powdered Milk

Hi Bob!

Selling Out

Wash Your Hair with Whipped Cream

The Bubble Wrap Book

Joey Green's Encyclopedia of Offbeat Uses for Brand-Name Products

The Warning Label Book

The Zen of Oz

Monica Speaks

The Official Slinky Book

You Know You've Reached Middle Age If...

The Mad Scientist Handbook

Clean Your Clothes

With Cheez Whiz®

AND HUNDREDS OF OFFBEAT USES FOR DOZENS MORE BRAND-NAME PRODUCTS

Joey Green

RENAISSANCE BOOKS
Los Angeles

Design by Joey Green

Cover credits: design by Lisa-Theresa Lenthall; photography by Marcel Eskenazy; model, Justeen Ward; hair and makeup by Jan Golden

Library of Congress Cataloging-in-Publication Data
Green, Joey.
    Clean your clothes with Cheez Whiz / Joey Green—1st ed
    p. cm.
    ISBN 1-58063-099-5 (alk. paper)
    1. Home economics. 2. Brand name products—United States. I. Title.
TX158.G6775 2000
640—dc21
                                                    00-034197

10 9 8 7 6 5 4 3
Published by Renaissance Books
Distributed by St. Martin's Press
Manufactured in the United States of America
First edition

For
Jeff, Suzy, and Audrey,
Lora, Barry, Henry, and Kim

Ingredients

But First, Another Word from Our Sponsor

In the 1970s, *Saturday Night Live* ran a fake commercial advertising a fictitious floor wax that doubled as a dessert topping—as a joke.

In the 1990s, I got Jay Leno to shave with Jif Peanut Butter, Rosie O'Donnell to condition her hair with Reddi-whip, and Conan O'Brien to mousse his hair with Miller High Life Beer—for real.

The moral? Truth is stranger than fiction. And the truth is: Corporate America keeps hundreds of fascinating alternative uses for brand-name products secret from the American public, compelling me to unearth these clandestine X-files and divulge the little-known uses for well-known products.

Once again I've discovered some astounding facts. Gatorade cleans toilets. French's Mustard soothes tired feet. Castor oil repels moles. Cool Whip relieves sunburn pain. But I wanted to know much more. How did Noxzema get its name? Who invented the Post-it Note? Who is Dr. Pepper, and where did he go to medical school?

This book is the result of my most daring expedition into the bowels of American ingenuity. True, I have yet to find a dessert topping that doubles as a floor wax. But I'm sure my experiments with Marshmallow Fluff will eventually yield impressive results—once I free my shoes from the kitchen floor.

Steak Sauce

■ **Shine shoes.** If you run out of shoe polish, use A.1. Steak Sauce on a soft cloth.

■ **Repair scratches on wood furniture.** Use a cotton ball to dab A.1. Steak Sauce on the scratch until achieving the right tone of brown.

■ **Relieve itching from insect bites.** Applying A.1. Steak Sauce over the affected areas alleviates itching.

■ **Remove tarnish from copper pots.** With a soft cloth, rub A.1. Steak Sauce on the tarnish. The acid from the tomato puree combined with the vinegar removes tarnish.

■ **Polish brass.** Apply A.1. Steak Sauce with a damp, clean cloth.

Invented
In the 1820s

The Name

Upon tasting the new sauce made by his royal chef, King George purportedly declared, "This sauce is A1!" During King George's reign (1820–1830), the phrase "A–number one"—or "A1" for short—became popular with the general public when Lloyds of London began rating ships for insurance purposes, with "A–number one" being the highest score. The sauce was again proclaimed "A.1." at international expositions in London in 1862 and 1880 and in Paris in 1867, 1878, 1889, and 1900.

A Short History

Henderson Brand, a Master Chef in the royal kitchens of King George IV of England, originally created A. 1. Steak Sauce, probably during the king's reign between 1820 and 1830. After the king's death in 1830, Brand resigned to go into business producing his sauce. In 1906, G. F. Heublein & Bros. began to export it to America. When World War I broke out and exports became impossible, Heublein acquired the manufacturing rights and began production in Hartford, Connecticut, in 1918. In 1936, Heublein purchased the rights to A.1. for $306,000. The company modified the flavor to suit the milder American palate, broadened its distribution, and has led the field ever since.

In 1982, Nabisco—founded in 1898 when Adophus Green consolidated several baking companies into the National Biscuit Company—acquired Heublein. Nabisco's history goes back to 1792, when Pearson & Sons Bakery in Massachusetts made "pilot bread," a tough and durable biscuit to sustain sailors on long journeys. Then, in 1801, the Josiah Bent Bakery baked a new product and called it a cracker. In 1889, believing that consolidation would improve quality and efficiency, Pearson, Bent, and six other bakeries united to form the New York Biscuit Company. In 1890, Adolphus Green formed the American Biscuit & Manufacturing Company, and, over the next eight years, combined approximately forty Midwestern bakeries to form the National Biscuit Company (later renamed Nabisco). R. J. Reynolds purchased Heublein in 1983. A.1. then became part of Nabisco with the merger of RJR and Nabisco. In 1999, Nabisco Inc. was spun off from RJR, and now trades as a separate entity on the New York Stock Exchange.

Ingredients

Tomato puree (water, tomato paste), distilled vinegar, corn syrup, salt, raisin paste, spices and herbs, crushed orange puree, dried garlic and onion, caramel color, potassium sorbate (to preserve freshness), xanthian gum

Strange Facts

■ During Prohibition, Heublein ceased all production of liquor and relied completely on sales of A.1. Steak Sauce to keep the company afloat.

Distribution

■ In 1998, Nabisco generated sales of $8.4 billion.
■ Nabisco sells its products in more than 150 countries around the world.
■ Nabisco also sells Barnum's Animal Crackers, Beech-Nut Gum, Breath Savers, Bubble Yum, Care-Free Gum, Cheese

Nips, Chips Ahoy!, Cream of Wheat Cereal, Grey Poupon Mustard, Honey Maid Graham Crackers, Knox Gelatin, Life Savers, Mallomars, Milk-Bone Dog Biscuits, Nilla Wafers, Now and Later, Nutter Butters, Oreo Cookies, Planters Peanuts, Ritz Crackers, Royal Gelatin, Snackwell's, Stella D'Oro, Triscuits, and Wheat Thins.

■ For a free copy of the *A.1. Steak Sauce Recipe Book*, write to Nabisco Foods, Inc., 100 DeForest Avenue, East Hanover, NJ 07936.

For More Information

Nabisco Foods, East Hanover, NJ 07936. Or telephone 1-800-NABISCO. On the Internet, visit www.A1Steak.com or www.nabisco.com.

Baby Magic

Baby Powder

■ **Repel ants.** Sprinkle Baby Magic Baby Powder in cracks, along a windowsill, or under doors where ants enter. Ants will not walk through baby powder.

■ **Help rubber gloves slip on easily.** Sprinkle Baby Magic Baby Powder inside the gloves.

■ **Give your dog a dry shampoo.** Rub Baby Magic Baby Powder into your dog's fur, wait a few minutes, then brush out.

■ **Cure a squeaky floor-board.** Sprinkle Baby Magic Baby Powder into the crevices along the edges.

■ **Hide a stain on a white suit.** Rub Baby Magic Baby Powder into the stain.

■ **Clean grease from walls.** Sprinkle Baby Magic Baby Powder on a soft cloth and rub the spot until the grease disappears.

■ **Keep shoes and sneakers dry and comfortable.**
Dust the insides with Baby Magic Baby Powder.

■ **Prevent sticky sheets on a hot, summer night.**
Sprinkle Baby Magic Baby Powder between the sheets to
absorb perspiration.

■ **Give your hair a dry shampoo.** Work Baby Magic
Baby Powder into your hair, then brush out.

■ **Prevent white shirts from absorbing oil and grime.**
Lightly sprinkle Baby Magic Baby Powder on the shirt
before and after ironing.

■ **Clean sand off wet skin.** Sprinkle Baby Magic Baby
Powder on skin to remove moisture, and the sand virtually
falls off by itself.

■ **Untangle a chain necklace.** Dusting the chain with
Baby Magic Baby Powder will make it easier to untangle.

■ **Soften rough hands.** Apply Baby Magic Baby Powder as
you would hand lotion.

■ **Prevent friction burns when shaving your legs with
an electric razor.** Dust legs lightly with Baby Magic Baby
Powder before shaving.

Invented
1973

The Name

The Baby Magic name obviously suggests the magical properties of both the product and babies. Baby Magic Baby Powder is cornstarch powder used specifically to absorb moisture from babies' skin to prevent diaper rash.

A Short History

Founded in 1878 by the Mennen family, the privately owned Mennen Company, traditionally considered makers of men's toiletries, became a market leader in deodorant and baby products, spearheaded by the Mennen Speed Stick, the best-selling deodorant in America, and followed by a line of Baby Magic baby shampoos, powders, and lotions. By the late 1980s, the company had sales over $500 million annually. In 1992, the Mennen family and the company's management, faced with increasing competition from Procter & Gamble, Unilever, and L'Oréal, sold the Mennen Company to Colgate-Palmolive for more than $670 million. In 1999, Colgate-Palmolive sold the Baby Magic line to Playtex Products, Inc.

Ingredients

Cornstarch, sodium bicarbonate, aloe-vera gel, tricalcium phosphate, fragrance

Strange Facts

■ Baby Magic baby powders were the first baby powders to contain finely ground oatmeal to provide more absorbency and reduced dusting.

- Baby Magic Baby Powder is purportedly 45 percent more absorbent than any talcum powder.
- When powdering a baby, always shake the powder into your hand, then pat it on the baby. Shaking the powder directly on the baby may create a powder cloud of fine particles.
- Baby powder is used to absorb moistness from the diaper area and help prevent chafing, irritation, and redness.

Distribution

- The Baby Magic brand line includes Baby Shampoo, Baby Bath, Baby Bath with Aloe, Baby Lotion, Baby Lotion with Aloe, and Baby Oil.

For More Information

Playtex Products, Inc., 300 Nyala Farms Road, Westport, CT 06880. Or telephone 1-888-532-BABY. On the Internet, visit www.playtexbaby.com.

Bag Balm

■ **Soothe chapped lips.** Just rub on a dab of Bag Balm to keep lips moist.

■ **Soothe nipples made sore from breast-feeding.** Developed to soothe sore cow teats, Bag Balm also soothes human nipples. Simply rub on a dab of Bag Balm.

■ **Protect skinned knees.** Covering the abrasion with a dab of fresh, uncontaminated Bag Balm and a bandage keeps the scab soft so a child is less apt to pick it off, and it helps the wound heal faster.

■ **Soothe chapped hands.** Just rub on Bag Balm.

■ **Soothe saddle sores from horseback riding, bicycling, or motorcycling.** Simply rub Bag Balm on the tender area.

- **Help heal small injuries or rash chapping on cattle.** Rub in Bag Balm.

- **Soften hardened, dry, pinched, or contracted horse hoofs and quarter cracks.** Simply rub in Bag Balm.

- **Quicken healing of cuts, scratches, skin irritations, and paw abrasions in dogs and cats.** Just rub on Bag Balm.

- **Soothe and quicken healing of eczema.** Rub a small dab of Bag Balm on the affected area.

- **Soothe skin around a nose irritated by a cold.** Constantly blowing your nose with tissues? Gently coat the reddened skin with a dab of Bag Balm.

Invented
1899

The Name
Bag Balm is named for the fact that this balm is intended to be used as a salve on a cow's udder, also known as a "bag."

A Short History
Vermont farmers use Bag Balm on cows' udders made sore from milking. Bag Balm speeds the healing of bruised, sore, or injured teats. Flexible dilators packed in Bag Balm ointment help keep the teat canal open for easier milking.

Ingredients

8-hydroxyquinoline sulfate 0.3 percent, in a petrolatum, lanolin base

Strange Facts

■ Until recently there were more cows in Vermont than people.

■ Dairy cows typically give milk for five to six years, producing an average of 12,147 pounds of milk.

■ Holstein cows produce more milk than any other breed of cow, but their milk contains less butterfat than other breeds. (Butterfat is used to make butter.)

■ Wisconsin has the largest population of dairy cattle (with over 2.5 million cows), followed by New York, Minnesota, and California.

Distribution

■ Bag Balm is available in farm supply stores, veterinary supply stores, and some pharmacies and health-food stores. Bag Balm is available at most Ace Hardware, Walgreen's, CVS, Southern States, Thrifty Drug, Fred Meyer, Super Value, and Agway stores.

For More Information

Dairy Association Co, Inc., P.O. Box 145, Lyndonville, VT 05851. Or telephone 1-800-232-3610. On the Internet, visit www.bagbalm.com.

Campbell's

Tomato Soup

■ **Prevent blond hair from turning green in a chlorinated swimming pool.** Rub Campbell's Tomato Soup into your hair after swimming.

■ **Get rid of the odor from a new permanent.** Saturate your hair with Campbell's Tomato Soup, cover your hair with a plastic shower cap, wait fifteen minutes, then rinse well and shampoo thoroughly.

■ **Eliminate skunk odor.** Pour several cups of Campbell's Tomato Soup into your bath water and soak for fifteen minutes, sponging it over your face. For skunk odor on pets, use rubber gloves to avoid getting the skunk odor on you, pour Campbell's Tomato Soup over your pet, and rub it in. Sponge it over the pet's face. Rinse and repeat.

■ **Tenderize meat.** Soak the meat in Campbell's Tomato Soup. The acids in tomatoes tenderize meat.

■ **Clean garlic, onion, or fish odors from hands.** Wash your hands with Campbell's Tomato Soup.

■ **Clean tarnish from copper pots.** Rub copper pots with Campbell's Tomato Soup.

■ **Clean tarnish from brass.** Rub brass with Campbell's Tomato Soup.

■ **Cook with Campbell's Tomato Soup.** The Campbell Soup Company publishes recipes for Tomato Soup Spice Cake, Campbell's Beef Taco Bake, Skillet Sweet & Tangy Chicken, and Fiesta Chicken & Rice Bake (each requiring one can of Campbell's Tomato Soup).

■ **Make a poor man's telephone.** Punch a small hole in the bottom of two clean, empty Campbell Soup cans. Then thread the ends of a long piece of string through the holes and tie each end to a button. You and a friend each take a can and walk apart until the string is straight and taut. Speak into the open end of your can. Your sound waves travel along the string and can be heard by your friend through the open end of the other can.

■ **Lock two bridge tables together.** Set the adjacent pairs of table legs inside clean, empty Campbell's Tomato Soup cans.

■ **Make a putting green in your backyard.** Punch a few holes each in the bottom of a few clean, empty Campbell's Tomato Soup cans and bury them in the grass. (The punched holes will allow water from rain or sprinklers to drain out.)

■ **Make an outdoor candle holder.** Punch holes in the sides of a clean, empty Campbell's Tomato Soup can, place a candle inside the can, and light.

■ **Prevent ants from climbing up a table when camping.** Fill four clean, empty Campbell's Tomato Soup cans halfway with water and set a table leg in each can. The ants won't be able to climb up the table.

■ **Store nails, screws, bolts, and washers.** Campbell's Soup cans make perfect storage containers.

■ **Make containers.** Spray a clean, empty Campbell's Tomato Soup can with a coat of spray paint. Glue several painted cans together with a glue gun to make a desk organizer for pencils and pens.

■ **Protect young garden plants from cutworms.** Remove the top and bottom from a clean, empty Campbell's Tomato Soup can, and push the can halfway into the earth around the plant.

■ **Make a funnel.** Using a can opener, punch a hole in the bottom side of a clean, empty Campbell's Tomato Soup can.

■ **Make candles.** A clean, empty Campbell's Tomato Soup can makes an excellent candle mold.

■ **Make a rain gauge.** Set a clean, empty Campbell's Tomato Soup can outside. An inch of water in the can means an inch of rainfall.

Invented

1897

The Name

Campbell Soup Company and the Campbell's brand are named after company founder Joseph Campbell.

A Short History

In 1869, fruit merchant Joseph Campbell, who made his mark selling soup from a horse-drawn wagon, teamed up with icebox manufacturer Abraham Anderson to start the Joseph A. Campbell Preserve Company in Camden, New Jersey, to produce canned tomatoes, vegetables, jellies, soups, condiments, and mincemeat. Anderson left the business in 1876 to start a rival company. In 1897, the Campbell Company's general manager, Arthur Dorrance, reluctantly hired his twenty-four-year-old nephew, Dr. John T. Dorrance, a chemist who had trained in Europe. The younger Dorrance was so determined to join Campbell that he agreed to buy his own laboratory equipment and accept a token salary of just $7.50 per week. The enthusiastic young chemist invented condensed soup. By eliminating the water in canned soup, he lowered the costs for packaging, shipping, and storage, enabling the company to offer a 10.5 ounce can of Campbell's condensed soup for a dime, versus more than 30 cents for a typical 32-ounce can of soup. In 1922, the Campbell Company formally adopted "Soup" as its middle name.

Ingredients

Tomato puree (water, tomato paste), wheat flour, sugar, salt, spice extract, citric acid

Strange Facts

■ The classic red-and-white Campbell's Soup can labels, immortalized by Andy Warhol in his classic Pop Art silk screens, were adopted in 1898, after a company executive named Herberton Williams attended the traditional football game between Cornell University and the University of Pennsylvania. Williams was inspired by the dazzling new red-and-white uniforms of the Cornell University football team.

■ The circular seal on the Campbell's Soup can pictures a medal won at the Paris Exposition of 1900.

■ In 1904, Philadelphia illustrator Grace Wiederseim drew the cherubic Campbell's Soup Kids, modeling the chubby-faced kids after herself. Like the Campbell Soup Kids, Wiederseim had a round face, wide eyes, and a turned-up nose. Over the years, the Campbell Soup Kids grew taller and lost a little baby fat. The Campbell's Soup Kids were introduced in a series of trolley-car advertisements, as a way to appeal to working mothers.

■ The original label on cans of Campbell's canned tomatoes portrayed two men hauling a tomato the size of an icebox.

■ In the 1900s, the Campbell Company's first magazine advertisement boasted twenty-one varieties of soup, each selling for a dime.

■ In the 1930s, Campbell began sponsoring radio shows, introducing the familiar "M'm! M'm! Good!" jingle.

■ In the 1950s, the Campbell's Soup Kids first appeared in television commercials. Forty years later, the Campbell's Soup Kids were seen dancing to rap songs.

■ In 1916, a cookbook entitled *Helps for the Hostess* originated the idea to use condensed soup in recipes. After World War II, Campbell's home economists cooked up recipes for dishes like "Green Bean Bake" and "Glorified Chicken."

■ Today, Americans use more than 440 million cans of Campbell's Soup each year for cooking.

■ Combined, Americans consume approximately 2.5 billion bowls of Campbell's three most popular soups—Tomato Soup, Cream of Mushroom, and Chicken Noodle—each year.

■ Ronald Reagan, Johnny Carson, Jimmy Stewart, Orson Welles, Helen Hayes, Donna Reed, Robin Leach, George Burns, Gracie Allen, and John Goodman have all served as spokespeople for various Campbell products.

■ Besides "M'm! M'm! Good!," other Campbell tag lines that have infected America's collective consciousness include "Wow! I could've had a V8!," "Uh-oh, SpaghettiOs," and "Pepperidge Farm remembers."

Distribution

■ Campbell's Soup, the bestselling soups in the United States, are available in practically every country in the world.

■ Campbell's sells hundreds of varieties of soups, including Cream of Broccoli, Double Noodle, and Creamy Chicken Noodle, Healthy Request Soups, Chunky Soups, and Home Cookin' Soups.

■ The Campbell Soup Company also makes Pepperidge Farm breads, cookies, and crackers, Franco-American gravies and pastas, V8 vegetable juices, Swanson chicken, and Godiva chocolates.

For More Information

Campbell Soup Company, Campbell Place, Camden, NJ 08103. Or telephone 1-800-257-8443. On the Internet, visit www.campbellsoup.com.

Castor Oil

■ **Repel moles.** Mix one-half cup castor oil and two gallons of water, and drench the molehills.

■ **Polish patent-leather shoes.** Rub a few drops of castor oil over shoes.

■ **Relieve breast inflammation or help heal minor breast infections.** Fold a wool flannel cloth in half, then fold in half a second time. Saturate the cloth with cold-pressed castor oil, place on the breast, cover with a piece of plastic, and then apply a heating pad set on moderate (increasing the temperature to the hottest you can handle). Let sit for an hour. Repeat for three to seven days. Cold-pressed castor oil helps increase T11 lymphocyte function, which will help speed the healing of the infection.

■ **Remove warts.** Apply a drop of plain castor oil to the wart twice a day and then cover it snugly with a piece of first-aid tape. Or mix a thick paste of castor oil and baking soda, apply to the wart a couple of times a day, and cover with a bandage, glove, or sock.

■ **Lubricate kitchen utensils.** Instead of petroleum oil, use castor oil on kitchen scissors and other utensils that will touch food.

■ **Relieve bursitis.** When the acute pain of bursitis subsides after four or five days, spread castor oil over the afflicted joint, place a piece of cotton or wool flannel over it, and apply a heating pad.

■ **Help prevent wrinkles around eyes.** Before going to bed, rub castor oil around your eyes.

■ **Relieve genital herpes.** Fold a wool flannel cloth in half, saturate with one cup castor oil, place on your belly, cover with a piece of plastic, and then apply a heating pad set on the highest setting you can handle, and let sit for an hour. Repeat daily for the first month, then three times a week. Increase the number of treatments during a herpes attack. Castor-oil packs strengthen your immune system, which then keeps the herpes virus from acting up.

■ **Soften dried leather shoes.** Using a sponge and warm water to dampen the outside of the shoes, then rub them with castor oil.

■ **Break in a new baseball glove.** Rub a few drops of castor oil into the palm of the glove, place a baseball in the glove, fold the mitt around it, and secure with rubber bands. Tuck the mitt under a mattress and leave overnight.

Invented
5000 B.C.E.

The Name
Castor oil is the yellowish *oil* extracted from the beans of the *castor*-bean plant, *Ricinus communis*, which is a native of tropical Africa that grows up to fifteen feet tall.

A Short History
Castor oil was first used as a laxative and skin softener throughout Mesopotamia and ancient Egypt. Ancient engineers also used castor oil as a lubricant for sliding giant stone blocks over wooden rollers.

Ingredients
100-percent castor oil

Strange Facts
■ Some pregnant women who are eager to induce labor drink castor oil mixed with orange juice to initiate contractions, but many doctors strongly advise against this practice. Castor oil can often work in a woman ready to give birth to stimulate labor by irritating the intestine into contractions (creating a corresponding reflex contraction in the uterine muscles). However, castor oil can cause uncontrolled uterine activity, spasmodic, painful contractions, and hyperstimulation of the uterus, which can result in fetal distress, the

passage of meconium into the uterus, and increased risk of intervention.

■ When chewed or broken and then swallowed, the seeds from the fruit of the castor-bean plant are poisonous to people, animals, and insects. Just one milligram of ricin, the main toxic protein in the castor bean, can kill an adult.

■ In 1978, ricin was used to assassinate Georgi Markov, a Bulgarian journalist who spoke out against the Bulgarian government. Markov was stabbed with the point of an umbrella while waiting at a bus stop near Waterloo Station in London. Doctors found a perforated metallic pellet, presumably containing the ricin toxin, embedded in his leg.

■ When castor beans are pressed to extract the castor oil, the toxin ingredient ricin is easily separated from the oil because it is water-soluble.

■ Oxidized castor oil—polymerized to increase viscosity and specific gravity—is used as a plasticizer in lacquers, inks, adhesives, rubber, and lubricants.

Distribution

■ Castor oil is available in drugstores everywhere.

■ Castor-bean plants grow in many tropical countries, primarily in Brazil and India. The oil is most widely used in industrial processes—to prepare foods, manufacture paints and dyes, and lubricate boat and airplane engines.

Cheerios

■ **Relieve itching from chicken pox, poison ivy, poison oak, or pain from sunburn.** Pour two cups Cheerios in a blender and blend into a fine powder on medium-high speed. Put the powdered Cheerios into a warm bath and soak in the oats for thirty minutes. It's a soothing oatmeal bath.

■ **Give yourself a moisturizing facial.** Make a paste from ground-up Cheerios, lemon juice, and honey. Apply to face, let sit for ten minutes, then rinse with warm water.

■ **Relieve dry, chapped hands.** Place one cup of Cheerios in a blender and blend into a very fine powder. Empty the powder into a large bowl. Rub your chapped

hands in the powder, gently removing the top layer of dead skin cells. Rinse with cool water, pat dry, and then apply hand cream.

■ **Help fight heart disease.** Beta-glucan—a soluble bran-based fiber found in whole oats, oat bran, and oat flour—can reduce serum cholesterol, a major risk factor in heart disease. A one-cup bowl of the traditional version of Cheerios in the bright yellow box contains 1 gram of beta-glucan soluble fiber, no more than 2 grams of fat, and zero saturated fat—which qualifies it for the FDA-approved claim that eating Cheerios, in conjunction with a diet low in saturated fats and cholesterol, can reduce the risk of heart disease. Data suggests very strongly that you need at least 3 and 4 grams of beta-glucan a day to see a significant cholesterol-lowering effect. That's equal to three cups of Cheerios every day. (A diet high in fat can negate any benefits from the oats.)

■ **Make Cheerios Treats.** Grease a 13- by 9-inch pan. Microwave three tablespoons margarine (or vegetable-oil spread) in a large, microwaveable bowl on high for 45 seconds or until melted. Add one package miniature marshmallows (six cups) or forty large marshmallows. Toss to coat with margarine or spread. Microwave on high for 45 seconds, stir, then microwave for another 45 seconds (or until smooth when stirred). Stir in one-half cup smooth or crunchy peanut butter. Immediately add five cups Cheerios cereal. Mix until well coated. Using greased spatula or wax paper, press mixture into prepared pan. Cool. Cut into squares. Makes about 24. (You can also mix one cup M&M's Chocolate Candies or one cup raisins and one-half cup dry roasted peanuts with cereal; add to warm marshmallow-peanut mixture.)

■ **Make "Cheerios Chicken."** Preheat oven to 400 degrees Fahrenheit. Line a jelly-roll pan (15.5 inches by 10.5 inches by 1 inch) with aluminum foil. Mix two cups finely crushed Cheerios (from the yellow box), one-quarter teaspoon pepper, one teaspoon parsley flakes, one-quarter teaspoon garlic powder, one-quarter teaspoon dried oregano leaves, and one-half teaspoon salt. Dip four chicken-breast halves (skinned and boned) into one-quarter cup milk, then roll in the cereal mix until well coated. Place the chicken in the pan and drizzle with two tablespoons melted margarine. Bake until done, about twenty to twenty-five minutes. (Above 3,500-foot elevation, bake about thirty minutes.) Makes four servings.

Invented
1941

The Name
These cheery O-shaped puffed oats were originally named Cheeri Oats until 1945, when the Quaker Oats Company claimed to own the exclusive right to use the word *oats* in a commercial name. To avoid legal action, General Mills quickly changed the name of Cheeri Oats to Cheerios.

A Short History
Developed by General Mills in 1941 as a convenient alternative to hot oatmeal, Cheeri Oats—America's first oat-based, ready-to-eat cereal—became an instant success, selling 1.8 million cases in its first year on the market.

In 1945, Cheeri Oats were renamed Cheerios. In 1979, General Mills introduced a second Cheerios variety—Honey Nut Cheerios. Naturally sweetened, with the taste of nuts and honey, Honey Nut Cheerios quickly became General Mills' second-bestselling cereal, behind the original Cheerios. In 1988, the company launched Apple Cinnamon Cheerios, which became one of America's top twenty bestselling breakfast cereals within two years. The company introduced Multi-Grain Cheerios in 1992, followed by Frosted Cheerios in 1995, and Team Cheerios in 1997.

Ingredients

Whole grain oats (includes the oat bran), modified food starch, sugar, salt, oat fiber, trisodium phosphate, calcium carbonate, vitamin E (mixed tocopherols, added to preserve freshness)

Strange Facts

■ Each little oat-based Cheerios O is individually puffed, one O at a time. Like popcorn, each Cheerios O explodes from the barrel of a puffing gun at a high temperature and a very high speed.

■ Cheeri O'Leary, the original Cheeri Oats mascot, appeared in ads during World War II and suggested seven nutritious "fighting breakfasts" built around Cheeri Oats.

■ Cheerios sponsored *The Lone Ranger* on radio from 1941 through 1949. Whenever the masked man righted a wrong, a radio announcer reminded listeners of the essential goodness of toasted whole-grain oats. Before riding off on his horse Silver, the Lone Ranger frequently touted Cheerios and then left behind his trademark silver bullet. In 1949, when the Lone Ranger and his faithful companion, Tonto, moved to television, Cheerios boxes contained a free silver bullet and offered *Lone Ranger* flashlight pistols for just 10 cents and one yellow boxtop.

■ From 1953 to 1973, television commercials for Cheerios featured the Cheerios Kid, who rescued his friend Sue from cartoon-world dangers. Whenever the Kid was "feelin' his Cheerios," a Cheerios O would burst forth from beneath his biceps.

■ Cheerios is the only ready-to-eat cereal clinically proven to reduce cholesterol when eaten as part of a hearty and healthy diet.

■ In the Disney movie *Honey, I Shrunk the Kids*, the shrunken kids wind up in a bowl of Cheerios. You can climb on giant Cheerios in the *Honey, I Shrunk the Kids* Adventure Zone at the Disney-MGM Studios Theme Park in Orlando, Florida.

Distribution

■ If every Cheerios O sold each year were laid end-to-end, they would make a line 21 billion feet long. That's over eight round-trips to the moon.

■ Cheerios is General Mills' bestselling, ready-to-eat cereal.

■ The Cheerios brand—including Cheerios, Apple Cinnamon Cheerios, Frosted Cheerios, Honey Nut Cheerios, Multi Grain Cheerios, and Team Cheerios—is the bestselling brand of ready-to-eat cereal in the United States.

■ In the United States, four boxes of Cheerios are sold every second.

■ Nearly 25 percent of all the Cheerios produced are eaten by children age five and under.

- Cheerios is one of the most popular cereals among adults older than forty-five.
- In 1996, General Mill sold more than $300 million worth of traditional Cheerios (in the yellow box).
- Besides Cheerios, General Mills—the second-largest cereal manufacturer in the United States—also makes Cocoa Puffs, Golden Grahams, Kix, Lucky Charms, Raisin Nut Bran, Total, Trix, Wheaties, Bisquick, Bugles, Fruit Roll-Ups, Hamburger Helper, Nature Valley Granola Bars, Pop Secret Microwave Popcorn, Potato Buds Instant Mashed Potatoes, and Yoplait Yogurt.

For More Information

General Mills, Inc., Box 1113, Minneapolis, MN 55440. Or telephone 1-800-328-6787. On the Internet, visit www.cheerios.com.

Cheez Whiz

■ **Clean grease from clothes.** Rub a dollop of Cheez Whiz into the grease stain and run through a regular wash cycle with detergent. The enzymes in Cheez Whiz will help loosen the grease stain.

■ **Fight plaque.** According to studies done by the Dow Institute for Dental Studies at the University of Iowa, eating 5 grams of cheddar cheese (less than an ounce) before meals eliminates the acid production of plaque.

■ **Make Cheez Whiz burgers.** Use Cheez Whiz instead of sliced cheese on your cheese burger.

■ **Condition hair and prevent split ends and frizzies.** Massage Cheez Whiz into dry hair, cover with a shower cap for thirty minutes, then shampoo and rinse thoroughly.

■ **Make Cheez Whiz dip.** Microwave one cup Cheez Whiz on medium for one minute, stir well, then heat for one more minute. Remove from microwave, stir well, and pour over nachos, tacos, or burritos. For more zest, stir a few drops of Tabasco Pepper Sauce into the melted Cheez Whiz.

■ **Shave.** If you run out of shaving cream, slather on Cheez Whiz.

Invented
1952

The Name
Cheez Whiz is obviously a misspelling of the word *cheese* combined with the word *whiz*, which describes a person with remarkable skill, such as the consumer with the wisdom to use this incredible product.

A Short History
In 1903, James Lewis Kraft started J. L. Kraft and Bros. Co., a cheese wholesaling business in Chicago. After developing Kraft Singles (individually wrapped slices of cheese), Kraft scientists formulated Cheez Whiz, a spreadable cheese product with its own distinct flavor, the ability to melt smoothly without clumping, and a cheerful orange color, slightly more pale than cheddar cheese. In 1992, forty years after the launch of Cheez Whiz, Kraft introduced Lite Cheez Whiz.

Ingredients

Cheese, milk, bacterial culture, salt, rennet and/or microbial enzyme, calcium chloride, lipase, water, modified milk ingredients, disodium phosphate, salt, seasoning, mustard flour, sorbic acid, color (A116C)

Strange Facts

■ Cheez Whiz has no aroma.

■ After Cheez Whiz has been melted down in a microwave, it will not resolidify.

■ Unlike most natural cheeses, Cheez Whiz is spreadable.

■ President George Bush enjoyed snacking on pork rinds in Tabasco Pepper Sauce, Shredded Wheat mixed with crushed Butterfinger bars, and pigs-in-a-blanket smothered with Cheez Whiz.

■ The advent of the microwave oven dramatically rejuvenated interest in Cheez Whiz because of its wonderful ability to microwave so gooily.

Distribution

■ Cheez Whiz flavors include Plain, Jalapeno, and Mild Salsa.

For More Information

Kraft Foods, Inc., White Plains, NY 10625. Or telephone 1-800-634-1984. On the Internet, visit www.cheezwhiz.com.

Clean Shower

■ **Clean blood from a white shirt.** Spray both sides of the garment with Clean Shower, let it sit for twenty-four hours, then launder in the regular cycle with detergent.

■ **Prolong the life of safety razor blades.** Squirt a little Clean Shower on a safety razor blade after each use. Some users report this triples the life of the razor.

■ **Clean countertops.** Spray Clean Shower on countertops and wipe it off a few moments later.

■ **Clean windows, mirrors, and glass.** Apply Clean Shower directly to the glass, wipe it off, spray the surface down with water, and wipe clean.

■ **Clean sinks and chrome fixtures.** Simply spray on Clean Shower, let it sit twenty minutes, and wipe clean.

■ **Clean mineral deposits from an enamel pot.** Spray with Clean Shower, let sit for three hours, then rinse thoroughly.

■ **Clean mold and mildew from plastic porch furniture.** Spray the furniture and the pads with Clean Shower and wipe clean. Then spray a light mist and do not wipe off, for added prevention.

■ **Clean a toilet.** Spray Clean Shower inside the bowl and under the seat, then brush and flush.

■ **Clean a bathtub.** Spray with Clean Shower, rub, and rinse.

■ **Clean bathroom stools.** Spray on some Clean Shower and wipe clean.

■ **Clean limestone deposits from a stainless-steel sink.** Spray on Clean Shower, wait a minute, then wipe off with a soft towel.

■ **Clean the dishwasher and washing machine.** Spray on Clean Shower, wait five minutes, then wipe off.

■ **Clean venetian blinds.** Spray on a little at a time and wipe off with a soft, clean cloth.

■ **Clean grout.** Spray on Clean Shower and wipe clean.

■ **Clean linoleum floors.** Mop the floor with water, then spray the floor with Clean Shower, and then mop it up.

■ **Open an clogged drain.** Pour Clean Shower down the drain of a shower or sink, let it sit for one hour, then flush with hot water.

■ **Clean household appliances.** Spray with Clean Shower and wipe off.

■ **Clean spots on carpet.** Spray Clean Shower on the stain, rub with a wet sponge, and let dry.

■ **Clean an oven.** Spray on Clean Shower, wait five minutes, spray it on again, and wipe off.

■ **Clean vinyl siding and ceilings.** Spray on Clean Shower, wait fifteen minutes, then wipe off with a sponge and a bucket of warm water.

■ **Prevent mold in a refrigerator.** Spray with Clean Shower and let dry.

■ **Wash a car.** Spray on Clean Shower, then wash off with a hose.

■ **Clean hairbrushes and combs.** Spray with Clean Shower, let sit for five minutes, then rinse thoroughly in water.

■ **Wash dishes.** Spray on Clean Shower, wipe with a sponge, rinse thoroughly, and dry.

■ **Clean laundry.** Spray tough stains with Clean Shower, then launder the garment as usual.

■ **Wash a dog.** Spray the pet with Clean Shower, then rinse thoroughly with water.

■ **Remove rust from tools.** Spray with Clean Shower, let dry, then rinse clean and dry.

■ **Clean mildew from a convertible ragtop.** Spray on Clean Shower and let dry.

■ **Clean stuffed animals.** Spray the plush toys lightly with Clean Shower and let dry.

■ **Remove mildew stains from fiberglass boats.** Spray with Clean Shower, let sit for five minutes, then wipe clean.

■ **Clean hair spray off vanities and mirrors.** Spray on Clean Shower, let it set, then wipe off.

Invented
1993

Name
Clean Shower is named for the fact that this product can *clean* a *shower* stall.

A Short History
In 1993, Harriet Black asked her husband, the chemist, to scrub the persistent mildew causing a foul odor from the shower in their home in Jacksonville, Florida. The event

changed Bob Black's life forever. After trying all of the leading products on the market without success, Black developed invented Clean Shower in his garage so he and his wife would never have to scrub the shower again. By simply using a trigger spray bottle to mist the surfaces in the shower with his new rinsing agent after each shower, Black eliminated the need to rinse, wipe, scrub with harsh cleaning agents, and squeegee. Instead, non-toxic, environmentally safe Clean Shower gets rid of soap scum, hard-water deposits, and mildew stains. The rinsing agents in Clean Shower stop the growth of mold and mildew on contact and prevent them from building up.

The Blacks shared Clean Shower with friends and family, creating demand for major quantities of Clean Shower, and prompting Bob Black to patent the product and go into production—under the umbrella of Automation, Inc., his Jacksonville-based manufacturing company.

Ingredients

Isopropyl alcohol, diammonium EDTA, linear aliphatic, polyether non-ionic surfactant, ester-based odor agent, water

Strange Facts

■ Ironically, after inventing Clean Shower, Bob Black discovered that the odor in his shower had been caused by a leak behind the shower wall.

■ The key ingredient in Clean Shower is a food preservative—a salt of EDTA, commonly used to prevent mold and mildew in crackers and other dry foods. One molecule of EDTA grabs one atom of a hard-water deposit and makes it soluble, like sugar, so it can be rinsed away with the next shower.

■ Clean Shower also contains isopropyl alcohol, which opens cell walls of mildew and allows the EDTA to remove the mildew's food. The alcohol also acts like a liquid squeegee— forcing water to sheet off shower walls. The alcohol then evaporates.

■ A special surfactant in Clean Shower, similar to the kind in conditioning shampoos, softens deposits and surrounds them with a rinsable soluble coating.

■ Clean Shower contains an alcohol to expand the cell walls of the fungus, a surfactant to make the cells lose their calcium, and chelating agents that grab the calcium and other minerals, making them unavailable to the mold and mildew.

■ Clean Shower works safely on shower surfaces including tile, fiberglass, porcelain, cultured marble, corian, terrazzo, glass shower doors, plastic shower curtains, chrome-plated fittings, brass fittings, rubber, grout, and silicone caulk.

■ Clean Shower does not contain chlorine, bleach, compounds containing phosphorus, sodium, toxic metals, quaternary amines, carcinogenic compounds, or inorganic acids.

■ A bottle of Clean Shower lasts about four weeks when used once a day in the shower.

Distribution

■ Clean Shower is the bestselling shower cleaner in the United States.

■ With a budget of a mere $1 million to launch Clean Shower nationally, Paul Porter, president of Clean Shower's in-house advertising agency, convinced some 1,000 drive-time radio DJs—including Rush Limbaugh, Charles Osgood, and Don

Imus—to use the product in their own bathrooms and then, if they truly loved it, to ad-lib endorsements for the product on the air.

■ In 1987, Clean Shower—which had sold $153,560 worth in 1995, and over $16.8 million in 1997—sold over $85 million.

For More Information

Clean Shower, L.P., 11737 Central Parkway, Jacksonville, FL 32224. Or telephone 1-904-998-9888. On the Internet, visit www.cleanshower.com.

Cool Whip

■ **Shine your shoes.** Use a tablespoon of Cool Whip on your leather shoes, and shine.

■ **Soothe sunburn pain.** Spread Cool Whip on the sunburn, let sit for twenty minutes, then rinse clean with lukewarm water.

■ **Thaw frozen fish.** Place the frozen fish in a pan and cover with Cool Whip. The dessert topping eliminates the frozen taste, returning the fresh-caught flavor.

■ **Condition your hair.** Apply one-half cup Cool Whip to dry hair once a week as a conditioner. Leave on for thirty minutes, then rinse a few times before shampooing thoroughly.

■ **Clean plant leaves.** Using a soft cloth, wipe a dab of Cool Whip on each leaf.

■ Soothe the burn on the roof of your mouth from hot pizza. Fill your mouth with Cool Whip to coat the lesion.

■ Give yourself a moisturizing facial. Cool Whip helps moisten dry skin when applied as a face mask. Wait twenty minutes, then wash it off with warm water, followed by cold water.

■ Lighten coffee. Use a tablespoon of Cool Whip as a substitute for milk or cream in a cup of coffee.

■ Help heal a cold sore. Place a compress of Cool Whip on the cold sore to speed healing, then rinse with cool water.

■ Remove makeup. Wet face with lukewarm water, spread a handful of Cool Whip on face, rinse clean with lukewarm water, and blot dry.

■ Clean silver. Mix two cups Cool Whip, and one tablespoon Heinz White Vinegar or ReaLemon Lemon Juice. Let silver stand overnight in mixture, then rinse clean and dry thoroughly.

■ Treat minor burns. Rub Cool Whip into the burn. Let it sit for fifteen minutes, then wash off with cool water.

■ Shave. Apply Cool Whip to wet skin as a substitute for shaving cream.

■ Store leftovers. Use empty "Cool Whip" containers as a substitute for Tupperware.

■ **Mix paints.** Use empty Cool Whip containers to mix and store paints.

■ **Store game pieces.** Never lose dice, cards, playing pieces, and small toys again.

■ **Store crayons.** Keep crayons in an empty Cool Whip container.

■ **Store screws, nuts, and bolts.** Use empty Cool Whip canisters in the workshop to hold loose screws, bolts, nuts, nails, drill bits, and spare parts.

■ **Store crafts.** Organize ribbons, beads, glues, strings in empty Cool Whip containers.

■ **Improve marital relations.** Give new meaning to the phrase "dessert topping."

Invented
1965

The Name
Since General Foods could not legally refer to its non-dairy topping as a whipped cream or milk product, the company's advertising agency generated hundred of nebulous names, finally recommending "Cool Whip" as the non-crème de la non-crème.

A Short History

When General Foods researchers surveyed a random group of housewives in the 1960s, they discovered that the women all wished for the development of a processed dessert topping that came already whipped, required no preparation, could be spooned right onto a dessert, and tasted as good as whipped cream. General Foods' Technical Center developed the product within six months.

Ingredients

Water, hydrogenated coconut and palm-kernel oils, corn syrup, high-fructose corn syrup, sugar, sodium caseinate (a milk-derived ingredient), less than 1 percent of natural and artificial flavors, polysorbate 60, sorbitan monostearate (for uniform dispersion of oil), xanthan gum and guar gum (thickeners), beta carotene (for color)

Strange Facts

■ Oddly, Cool Whip is labeled as a "non-dairy whipped topping" despite the fact that it contains sodium caseinate, an ingredient derived from milk.

■ Sodium caseinate, a milk derivative in Cool Whip, is also used to make glue.

■ Stirring Cool Whip vigorously will cause the whipped topping to deflate and lose its airy texture.

■ Unlike whipped cream, Cool Whip lasts for up to two weeks thawed in the refrigerator.

■ In 1966, Cool Whip sponsored *The Andy Griffith Show*.

Distribution

■ Cool Whip is the bestselling whipped topping in the United States.

■ Cool Whip whipped toppings are available in four styles (Cool Whip Non-Dairy, Cool Whip Extra Creamy, Cool Whip Lite, and Cool Whip Free) that can be used interchangeably in recipes (but all will not perform equally in recipes).

■ Cool Whip holds a 70-percent share of the whipped-topping market.

■ According to the Market Research Institute, one out of three American homemakers buys Cool Whip regularly.

For More Information

Kraft Foods, Inc., Box CW-8, White Plains, NY 10625. Or telephone 1-800-431-1001. On the Internet, visit www.coolwhip.com.

Country Time

Lemonade

■ **Clean your dishwasher.** Fill the detergent cup with Country Time Lemonade powdered mix and run the machine through its normal cycle. The citric acid in Country Time Lemonade removes grunge and soap scum from the inside of a dishwasher.

■ **Dye wool from sheep before spinning it.** The acid in Country Time Lemonade helps cut through the lanolin on the wool and makes the dye take better.

■ **Clean a toilet bowl.** Pour in two tablespoons of Country Time Lemonade powdered mix. Let it stand for one hours. Brush and flush. The citric acid removes stains from porcelain.

■ **Shampoo your hair.** The citric acid in Country Time Lemonade cuts through sebum oil in hair.

■ **Spice up your baking.** Adding a pinch of Country Time Lemonade powdered mix to your cake and cookie mixes gives them a lemon kick.

■ **Make a Lemon Zinger.** Mix Country Time Lemonade with vodka.

Invented
1975

The Name
"Country Time" cleverly conjures up the image of sitting on a porch swing drinking a tall, refreshing glass of fresh lemonade in the country.

A Short History
Anticipating that there would be a huge market for an instant powdered lemonade-flavored drink mix, Kraft internally generated Country Time Lemonade, introducing ten-quart canisters of the product (with a measuring scoop packed inside) in regional markets in the Midwest in 1975. By the following year, Country Time Lemonade was available nationwide, in four-quart canisters as well.

Ingredients
Sugar, fructose, citric acid (provides tartness), magnesium oxide (prevents caking), natural flavor, salt

Strange Facts

■ The lemon is actually a type of berry called *hesperidium*.

■ Lemons are believed to have originated in northeastern Indian, near the Himalayas.

■ The first lemon trees in America were planted in 1493 by Christopher Columbus.

■Jack Lemmon's real last name is Lemmon.

■ The word *lemon* is slang for "a defective automobile," derived from the fruit's unavoidable sour taste.

■ The word *lemon* is also used as slang for a "Quaalude," after Lemmon, the pharmaceutical company that originally made the drug.

■ According to his memoirs, Casanova gave his mistresses partially squeezed lemon halves to use as cervical caps. The acidic juice acted as a spermicide.

Distribution

■ Country Time Lemonade varieties include Regular, Lem'N Berry Sippers, and Sugar Free.

For More Information

Kraft Foods, Inc., Box CTL-C6, Rye Brook, NY 10573. Or telephone 1-800-431-1002. On the Internet, visit www.kraftfoods.com.

Nail Polish Remover

■ **Dissolve Krazy Glue from skin.** Soak a cotton ball in Cutex Nail Polish Remover, hold it on the area until the glue dissolves, then wash thoroughly with soap and water.

■ **Remove scuffs from patent leather or white shoes.** Put Cutex Nail Polish Remover on a soft cloth or paper towel and rub lightly.

■ **Clean sneakers or gym shoes.** Put Cutex Nail Polish Remover on a clean cloth and rub the sneakers or gym shoes.

■ **Counter the affects of poison ivy.** Within thirty minutes of contact with poison ivy, wash the contaminated skin with soap and water, then use a cotton ball to apply Cutex Nail Polish Remover to the area. According to the *New York*

Times, the acetone in the nail-polish remover will remove some of the urushiol, the oil in poison ivy that rapidly penetrates the skin and combines with skin proteins to trigger an allergic reaction, thus reducing the severity of the itching and possibly preventing a rash altogether.

■ **Clean tools.** Put Cutex Nail Polish Remover on a clean cloth and wipe the tools.

■ **Remove ballpoint-pen ink or paint from skin.** Put Cutex Nail Polish Remover on a clean cloth, wipe the skin, then wash thoroughly with soap and water.

■ **Clean ink and other stains from countertops.** Put Cutex Nail Polish Remover on a clean cloth, wipe the stain, then wash thoroughly with soap and water.

■ **Remove temporary tattoos from skin.** Rub the "tattoo" with a cotton ball soaked in Cutex Nail Polish Remover, then wash thoroughly with soap and water.

■ **Remove burns on wood furniture.** Dip a Q-Tips Cotton Swab in Cutex Nail Polish Remover and gently rub over the burn.

■ **Clean scissors.** Soak a cotton ball in Cutex Nail Polish Remover and cautiously clean the scissor blades.

■ **Remove bumper stickers.** Soak a soft, clean cloth in Cutex Nail Polish Remover, place it on the bumper sticker, then peel off.

■ **Remove price tags from products.** Rub the price tag with a cotton ball soaked in Cutex Nail Polish Remover, then gently peel off the label. The acetone in the nail-polish remover dissolves the glue.

■ **Repair scratches on the plastic face of a wristwatch.** Dip a Q-Tips Cotton Swab in Cutex Nail Polish Remover and gently rub it over the face of the watch until the scratches vanish.

Invented
1916

The Name
Cutex is a hybrid of the word *cuticle* and the suffix *-ex*, to describe the company's original product—liquid cuticle remover.

A Short History
In 1911, pharmacist Northam Warren, the son of a minister, developed his liquid cuticle remover to make manicuring easier. Until then, manicurists cut and trimmed the cuticle with fine scissors, and manicures required up to two hours. Warren advertised his Cuticle Remover as a way to "make manicuring easier," and his revolutionary new product was praised by fashion magazines like *Vogue* and *Harper's Bazaar*. By 1912, most professional manicurists were using Warren's Cuticle Remover, as were hundreds of thousands of American woman who could now manicure their own nails.

In 1916, Warren introduced the first liquid nail polish in the United States and called it Cutex—immediately followed by the introduction of Cutex Nail Polish Remover.

Ingredients

Acetone, water, propylene carbonate, dimethyl glutarate, dimethyl succinate, dimethyl adipate, glycerin, diglycerol, gelatin, fragrance, yellow 11

Strange Facts

■ A solid-gold manicure set, dating back to 3200 B.C.E., was found in the royal tombs at Ur of the Chaldees in southern Babylonia.

■ Queen Nefertiti of Egypt, known as one of history's most beautiful women, painted her finger- and toenails a rich, ruby red.

■ Cleopatra painted her nails a deep, rusty shade of red.

■ In ancient Babylon and Rome, great warriors had their nails painted the same shade as their lips before going into battle.

■ When Northam Warren introduced Cuticle Remover in 1911, less than 25 percent of the women in the United States used any manicuring products at all. Today, 75 percent do.

■ During the Depression, Northam Warren launched an advertising campaign to introduce deeper and darker shades of nail polish, launching the fashion of brightly colored nails.

■ Rule 19 of the American Bowling Congress forbids the use of Cutex Nail Polish Remover for cleaning a bowling ball used in competitions.

■ The gelatin in Cutex helps add strength and resiliency to fingernails.

Distribution

■ Cutex is the bestselling brand of nail-polish remover in the world.

For More Information

MedTech, P.O. Box 1108, Jackson, WY 83001. Or telephone 1-800-443-4908.

Caulk

■ **Fix a hole in the sole of a shoe or sneaker.** Fill with DAP Caulk, let dry.

■ **Repair a torn refrigerator or dishwasher gasket.** Fill with DAP Caulk.

■ **Prevent cabinet doors from slamming shut.** Squirt a small bead of DAP Caulk at the top and bottom on the inside corners of each cabinet door. Place strips of Scotch Tape on the cabinet where the caulk makes contact, coat each piece of tape with a thin film of Vaseline Petroleum Jelly, and then tape a small piece of cardboard, approximately one-eighth of an inch thick, to the cabinet between the tape strips. Close the cabinet door, let the caulk dry overnight, then peel off the tape and cardboard.

■ **Seal plants.** Use DAP Caulk to seal ends of pruned stems and branches against insects and excessive moisture.

■ **Deter ants.** Follow a trail of ants into your house and seal off the point of entry with DAP Caulk.

Invented

1866

The Name

DAP stands for the last names of company founders Robert H. Dicks and George Pontius, and the Armstrong Company of Chicago, which merged with Dicks-Pontius Co. in 1957.

A Short History

In 1865, Robert H. Dicks, who had developed a sealing wax in his garage, teamed up with Elmer Wiggins to launch a company from Dayton, Ohio, to produce and market sealing wax for preserving food in canning jars. In 1906, Dicks partnered with George Pontius of Columbia City, Indiana, who was producing a similar product. Since sealing wax was a seasonal product, the Dicks-Pontius Company expanded to produce a line of putty and caulk products under the D-P label, selling these items in bulk to the construction trade. With the advent of canning jars with rubber-sealed lids, D-P business phased out its sealing-wax operations.

The post–World War II building boom prompted D-P to supply caulk products in disposable cartridges, eliminating the need to load caulk guns from bulk containers. In 1957, the Dicks-Pontius Co. merged with Armstrong Co. of Chicago to become D.A.P., eventually leading to the DAP brand name. The new company pioneered the development of vinyl spackling and became the world's largest manufacturer of putty and caulking compounds.

DAP then went through six changes in corporate ownership. In 1960, Plough, Inc., acquired DAP. In 1971, Plough merged with Schering, Inc., to become Schering-Plough. In 1983, Schering-Plough sold DAP to Beecham. In 1987, DAP Inc. became a subsidiary of USG Corporation. Three years later, DAP Inc. was acquired by Wassall PLC, and in 1999, DAP Inc. was bought by RPM, Inc., a publicly held company on the New York Stock Exchange.

Strange Facts

■ A wet Popsicle stick makes an excellent caulking trowel.
■ In a pinch, a chewed-up piece of Wrigley's Spearmint Gum makes an excellent caulk. (DAP Caulk, however, does not make a good substitute for a stick of Wrigley's Spearmint Gum.)
■ Silly Putty can also be used as temporary caulk around windows.

Distribution

■ DAP is the leading manufacturer of caulks, sealants, adhesives, wood preservatives, paints, repair products, floor-covering preparation products, and tile-installation products for the construction and do-it-yourself industries.
■ DAP products can be found throughout the world.

For More Information

DAP, Inc., Baltimore, MD 21224. Or telephone 1-888-DAP-TIPS. On the Internet, visit www.dap.com.

■ Remove grease from clothes. Empty a can of Dr Pepper into a load of greasy workclothes, add detergent, and run through a regular wash cycle. Dr Pepper will help loosen grease stains.

■ Clean corrosion from car battery terminals. Pour a can of carbonated Dr Pepper over the terminals to bubble away the corrosion.

■ Clean insects off a car windshield. Pour a can of carbonated Dr Pepper over the windshield and squeegee clean.

■ Clean a toilet bowl. Pour a can of Dr Pepper into the toilet bowl. Let it sit for one hour, then brush and flush clean. The citric acid in Dr Pepper removes stains from vitreous china.

■ Loosen a rusted bolt. Apply a cloth soaked in a carbonated Dr Pepper to the rusted bolt for several minutes.

■ Remove rust spots from chrome car bumpers. Rubbing the bumper with a crumpled-up piece of Reynolds

Wrap Aluminum Foil dipped in Dr Pepper will help remove rust spots.

■ **Cook with Dr Pepper.** Dr Pepper offers a free packet of recipes including Apple Muffins (with one cup of Dr Pepper), Peachy Chiffon Pie (with one-and-a-quarter cups of Dr Pepper), Jellied Grape Salad (with one-and-three-quarters cups of Dr Pepper), and Candied Sweet Potatoes (with one cup of Dr Pepper). For a free copy, call 1-800-527-7096.

■ **Make beef stew.** Sprinkle three pounds boneless stew meat (beef) with three teaspoons salt and one teaspoon black pepper and dust with one-quarter cup flour. In a large kettle, brown the meat in three tablespoons shortening until very brown. Add two cups beef stock or bouillon, two cups Dr Pepper, two cups sliced carrots, one-and-a-half cups onion chunks, and one cup sliced celery. Cook at a low temperature until meat is very tender. Add one cup frozen or fresh garden peas and cook at least ten minutes more. Makes 8 servings.

Invented
1885

The Name
Dr Pepper is purportedly named after a Virginia physician, Dr. William R. Pepper, whose daughter, Minerva, captured the heart of local pharmacist Wade B. Morrison. Customers at Morrison's Old Corner Drug Store in Waco, Texas, familiar with the story of the short-lived romance, named the bittersweet soft drink after Dr. Pepper.

A Short History

In 1885, Charles Alderton, a young pharmacist working at Wade Morrison's Old Corner Drug Store in the central Texas town of Waco, also served carbonated drinks at the soda fountain. Realizing that customers were tired of drinking the same old fruit flavors, he began experimenting with flavors of his own until he hit upon one he liked—which he tested on Wade Morrison, who also liked the new soft drink.

Alderton then offered his new drink to some of his soda-fountain customers. They liked it, too. Word spread, and soon everyone at Morrison's soda fountain was ordering the new soft drink, called a "Waco," because Waco was the only place it was available. Patrons suggested that Morrison name the new fountain drink after Dr. Pepper, the Virginia physician who purportedly refused to let Morrison marry his daughter. Legend holds that Wade Morrison later returned to Virginia and finally won the hand of Dr. Pepper's daughter, but, in reality, he married Carrie B. Jeffress in 1882 and remained married to her until his death in 1924.

Soon other soda-fountain operators in Waco began buying the syrup from Morrison and serving it. Morrison decided to bottle the drink, and in 1891 formed the Artesian Manufacturing and Bottle Company (named after the many artesian wells in the area that supposedly supplied healthful water). Robert S. Lazenby, a young beverage chemist hired to run the plant, perfected and stabilized the formula for bottling. Alderton, the soft drink's originator, remained more interested in the pharmacy than the soft-drink business.

In 1904, Lazenby introduced Dr Pepper to almost twenty million people attending the 1904 World's Fair Exposition in St. Louis. In 1923, Lazenby and his son-in-law, J. B. O'Hara, moved the company to Dallas and changed the name to the Dr Pepper Company. O'Hara eventually became president of the company and expanded sales throughout the United States. In 1986, the Dr Pepper Company merged with the Seven-Up Company to form Dr Pepper/Seven-Up Companies, Inc., which was acquired in 1995 by Cadbury Schweppes.

Ingredients

Carbonated water, high-fructose corn syrup and/or sugar, caramel color, phosphoric acid, artificial and natural flavors, sodium benzoate (preservative), caffeine

Strange Facts

■ Dr Pepper was invented one year before Coca-Cola (1886) and six years before Pepsi-Cola (1901).

■ The original formula for Dr Pepper did not contain caffeine or cocaine because some researchers at the time considered caffeine and cocaine dangerous, even though both substances were legal.

■ In 1917, Robert Lazenby, president of the company, decided to add caffeine to Dr Pepper. In 1939, Dr Pepper executives took the caffeine out and added vitamin B-1, reasoning that the drink would be healthier and therefore more popular. Unfortunately, the vitamin caused the soft drink to go bad and changed the taste. Vitamin B-1 was promptly taken out of Dr Pepper.

■ The original advertising slogan for Dr Pepper was "Liquid Sunshine."

■ Twenty-three fruit flavors make up Dr Pepper.

■ When Dr Pepper made its debut at the 1904 World's Fair Exposition in St. Louis, the exposition also marked the first time in history that hamburgers and hot dogs were served on buns. The exposition also witnessed the introduction of the edible ice cream cone.

■ In 1906, the Dr Pepper Company bought the Freckleater Company, which manufactured an ointment for removing freckles from the skin. In 1907, Dr Pepper sold the Freckleater Company back to its original owner for the same price it was purchased.

■ Dr Pepper Company is the oldest major manufacturer of soft-drink concentrates and syrups in the United States.

■ During the 1920s and 1930s, while Dr Pepper was sold by "Old Doc," a typical country-doctor character with monocle and top hat, Dr. Walter Eddy, a professor at Columbia University, discovered that the average person experiences a slump of energy during the normal day at 10:30 A.M., 2:30 P.M., and 4:30 P.M. Since research also showed that the sugar in Dr Pepper provided energy, J. B. O'Hara originated the famous advertising slogan, "Drink a bite to eat at 10, 2, and 4," which was eventually abbreviated to the mysterious "10-2-4" on the bottles.

■ Dr Pepper's advertising slogans have included "If Atlas were on earth, he would recommend Dr Pepper," and "It leaves a pleasant farewell and a gracious call back."

■ The period after "Dr" was dropped in 1950.

■ In the 1960s, Dr Pepper, "the friendly Pepper-Upper," sponsored Dick Clark's *American Bandstand* television show.

■ In 1963, Dr Pepper introduced "Dietetic Dr Pepper," but changed the name three years later after realizing that people confused the word *dietetic* with *diabetic*.

- Dr Pepper went from being "the most misunderstood soft drink" in the 1960s, to "the most original soft drink ever" in the 1970s.
- In 1977, Dr Pepper launched the famous "Be a Pepper" commercial jingle, prompting *Saturday Night Live* to do a sketch starring Bill Murray leading the Not Ready for Prime Time Players as Peppers.
- In 1991, the Dr Pepper Museum and Free Enterprise Institute opened in the classic 1906 "Richardsonian Romanesque" building in downtown Waco, Texas, that served as the national headquarters for Dr Pepper until 1922. The building stands three blocks from the original site of Morrison's Old Corner Drug Store, where Dr. Charles Alderton first created Dr Pepper in 1885. The building is the only surviving early headquarters for a major American soft drink. Aside from showcasing the history of Dr Pepper, the museum boasts one of the largest soft-drink collections in the world, a working antique soda fountain, and a gift shop with a catalog offering more than 1,500 items.

Distribution

- Dr Pepper, the oldest of the major-brand soft drinks in America, sold nearly 900 million gallons in 1998.
- Diet Dr Pepper, reformulated in 1991, is the number one–selling diet non-cola in the United States.

For More Information

Dr Pepper/Seven-Up Companies, Inc., P.O. Box 869077, Plano, TX 75086-9077. Or telephone 1-800-527-7096. On the Internet, visit www.drpepper.com.

Formula 409

■ **Kill flies.** Spraying Formula 409 at flies kills them.

■ **Remove a ring stuck on a finger.** Spray the ring with Formula 409 and it will slide right off, then rinse the ring and your hands thoroughly.

■ **Clean white rings from furniture.** Spray Formula 409 on a soft cloth, rub the stain, and wipe off.

■ **Polish leather shoes.** Spray on Formula 409 and shine with a cloth.

■ **Remove spots from carpet.** Apply Formula 409 to the stain, rub it in, wait a few minutes, blot up stain, then rinse well.

■ **Prevent tarnish on brass.** Spray Formula

409 on a soft cloth, rub the brass, let dry, then rub lightly with polish.

■ **Clean a barbecue grill.** While the grill is still warm, spray with Formula 409, and scrub clean with a metal brush.

■ **Mist plants.** Fill a clean, empty Formula 409 bottle with water and mist your houseplants.

Invented
1936

The Name
Formula 409 was developed on its 409th try.

A Short History
In 1910, Cincinnati-based Philip Drackett began distributing bulk industrial chemicals formulated and packaged for use in institutional settings. In 1923, after Drackett's son, H. R., invented Drano, the company expanded into consumer products—followed by the inventions of Formula 409, Vanish, and Mr. Muscle. In 1963, entrepreneur Wilson L. Harrell, a native of Jacksonville, Florida, bought the bankrupt Formula 409 Inc. for $30,000. Harrell persuaded television celebrity Art Linkletter to invest $85,000 in the company and be a spokesman for the product. By 1971, Formula 409 was the bestselling cleaning product of its kind in the nation. In 1972, Harrell sold Formula 409 to the Clorox Company for $7 million.

Ingredients

Isopropanol, 2-butoxyenthanol, surfactants, fragrance

Strange Facts

■ The cleaning agents in Formula 409 are biodegradable.

■ In 1993, *Fortune* named the Clorox Company a Top Ten United States environmental leader.

■ In 1957, Procter & Gamble bought Clorox, resulting in antitrust litigation by the FTC for the next decade. Procter & Gamble was ordered to divest itself of Clorox, and in 1969, Clorox again became an independent company.

Distribution

■ The Clorox Company sells its products in ninety-four countries and produces them in more than thirty plants in the United States, Puerto Rico, Canada, Mexico, Argentina, and South Korea.

■ The Clorox Company also manufactures Brita Water Filtering Systems, Clorox Bleach, Clorox Clean-Up Cleaner, Clorox 2 All-Fabric Bleach, Combat Insect Control Systems, Fresh Step Cat Litter, Hidden Valley Ranch Salad Dressing, K. C. Masterpiece Barbecue Sauce, Kingsford Charcoal Briquets, Kitchen Bouquet Browning and Seasoning Sauce, Liquid-Plumr Drain Opener, Pine-Sol Cleaner, Soft Scrub Mild Abrasive Liquid Cleanser, Stain Out Soil and Stain Remover, and Tilex Mildew Remover. Other brands include Glad, Johnny Cat, Armor All, and STP.

■ In 1999, the Clorox Company's sales topped $4 billion.

For More Information

The Clorox Company, 1221 Broadway, Oakland, CA 94612-1888. On the Internet, visit www.clorox.com.

Clothes Pins

■ **Prevent a retractable vacuum-cleaner cord from springing back into the machine.** Clip a Forster Clothes Pin to the electrical cord at the length you desire.

■ **Remember to turn off your headlights during the day.** When you turn on your headlights in the daytime, clip a Forster Clothes Pin to your keys. This way, you'll remember to turn the lights off again when you get out of the car.

■ **Replace spark plugs with ease.** Before disconnecting the spark-plug cables, number Forster Clothes Pins with a Magic Marker and clip to each cable.

■ **Hold wires in place while soldering.** Use a Forster Clothes Pin.

■ **Organize cables and extension cords.** Clip the cords together with Forster Clothes Pins.

■ **Identify badly soiled clothes.** Keep a basket of Forster Clothes Pins near the laundry bin and instruct family members to clip one to any garment that needs special attention in the wash.

■ **Secure plants to a trellis.** Simply clip the plant to the trellis with a Forster Clothes Pin.

■ **Seal open bags of potato chips or pretzels.** Use a Forster Clothes Pin to clip the bags closed.

■ **Hem fabric when sewing.** Instead of basting the fabric with pins, clip the hemline with Forster Clothes Pins.

■ **Identify plants.** With a Forster Clothes Pin, clip the papers identifying the name of the plant, the number of seeds, and the date planted to the pot.

■ **Give your bicycle the roar of a motorcycle.** Use Forster Clothes Pins to clip playing cards to the beams that hold the bicycle wheels in place so that the cards are held poking into the spokes.

■ **Hang Christmas lights.** Use Forster Clothes Pins to clip strings of Christmas lights to your house.

■ **Post reminder notes in your car.** Clip a reminder to the sun visor with a Forster Clothes Pin.

■ **Make shopping with coupons easier.** Bring a Forster Clothes Pin to the supermarket when you go shopping and clip it to the shopping cart. When you find an item in the grocery store that you have a coupon for, clip the coupon in the Forster Clothes Pin. This way, when you get to the checkout counter, you'll have all your coupons ready.

■ **Prevent picnic tablecloths from blowing away.** Hold the corners to the table with Forster Clothes Pins.

■ **Hold a leaf bag open when raking leaves.** Use two or three Forster Clothes Pins to clip one side of a plastic trash bag to a chain-link fence. This way, you can hold the other side open to fill it with leaves easily.

■ **Organize boots.** Clip your left and right boots together with a Foster Clothes Pin so they stay together in the closet.

■ **Keep a recipe card accessible.** Clip the recipe card you're using to a cabinet door with a Forster Clothes Pin to keep it at eye level and clean. You can also glue or screw the clothes pin to a nearby surface to make a permanent holder.

■ **Repair clothes in an emergency.** A Forster Clothes Pin will hold fabric together until you can find a needle and thread.

■ **Seal open bags of frozen food.** Use a Forster Clothes Pin to clip bags of frozen vegetables closed.

■ **Improvise a paintbrush.** Clip a Forster Clothes Pin to a small square of sponge or foam rubber.

■ **Improvise a bib for children.** Use a Forster Clothes Pin to clip a dish towel around the child's neck.

■ **Hold pleats in place while ironing.** Use Forster Clothes Pins.

■ **Keep drapes away from air conditioners.** Clip several Forster Clothes Pins to the inside of the drapes to distance them from the air conditioner.

■ **Clip together papers.** Use a Forster Clothes Pin to secure papers together.

■ **Prevent milk from absorbing odors in the refrigerator.** Clip the milk carton shut with a Forster Clothes Pin.

■ **Help children play cards.** Use a Forster Clothes Pin to clip a hand of playing cards together so children can hold them more easily.

■ **Make a pot of tea.** Clip the strings of several tea bags together with a Forster Clothes Pin, place the tea bags in the tea pot, and let the clothes pin hang over the lip of the pot.

Invented

1938

The Name

Forster is named after company founder Charles Forster. The clothes pin was named for the purpose of the small clip—to pin clothes to a clothesline.

A Short History

In the 1800s, the toothpick—commonly made of ivory, quill, or a precious metal—was carried by the individual, much like a pocket comb. While traveling through Brazil, Boston native Charles Forster learned that Brazilians had been whittling toothpicks from pieces of orange trees for generations. In 1869, Forster built the first toothpick workshop in the cellar of his Boston home, determined to manufacture the first commercially produced wooden toothpick.

When restaurants refused to sell his new product, Forster hired several suave, successful-looking young men to visit prominent Boston restaurants where, after finishing an elegant dinner, they would ask for disposable toothpicks. When they were told there were none to be had, they demanded to see the manager and protested loudly. To quiet the indignant gentlemen, restaurant managers would ask if these toothpicks could be purchased, giving birth to Forster, Inc.

In 1887, Forster began the first wooden toothpick factory in the United States. Fifty years later, the company began manufacturing round, square, and springed clothes pins. In 1995, Diamond Brands acquired Forster.

Ingredients

White birch, galvanized steel

Strange Facts

■ Crafted in Maine, Forster Clothes Pins grip tighter, open wider, and stay together longer than any other clothes pin. They also resist rust.

■ The disposable wooden toothpick can be found in nearly every home and eating establishment across the United States.

Distribution

■ Forster Clothes Pins are the bestselling clothes pins in the United States.
■ Forster produces 7.2 billion toothpicks, 2.1 billion pieces of plastic cutlery, and 400 million clothes pins annually.
■ Forster makes Large Spring Clothes Pins, Small Spring Clothes Pins, Mini-Spring Clothes Pins, and Tiny Spring Clothes Pins.

For More Information

Forster Manufacturing Company, Inc., P.O. Box 657, Wilton, ME 04294. Or telephone 1-207-645-2574. On the Internet, visit www.diamondbrands.com/forster.html.

Mustard

■ **Prevent hens from eating their own eggs.**
Paint a little French's Mustard on the eggshell.

■ **Deodorize a bottle.** Mix two teaspoons
French's Mustard with one quart water.
Rinse well.

■ **Get kids to eat their food.** Let
children use a squeeze bottle of
French's Mustard to make funny
faces on hamburgers, hot dogs, and
sandwiches—to make mealtime
funtime, and encourage children
to eat their artistic creations.

■ **Relieve the symptoms of
arthritis.** Rub French's Mustard into your hands.

■ **Soothe tired feet.** Fill a pan
with warm water and mix in three
tablespoons French's Mustard.

■ **Spice up pretzels.** Squeeze French's Mustard onto a
large, soft pretzel, or dip pretzels in French's Mustard for a
tangy treat.

■ **Relieve the symptoms of a cold.** Rub French's Mustard on your chest.

■ **Soothe sore muscles.** Apply a poultice of French's Mustard.

■ **Take a mustard bath.** Spoon six tablespoons of French's Mustard and a handful of Epsom salts into the bathtub as it fills.

■ **Make mustard-vinaigrette salad dressing.** Whisk together one-quarter cup red-wine vinegar and three tablespoons French's Mustard. Gradually whisk in two-thirds cup olive oil. Season to taste with salt and pepper. Makes one cup.

■ **Soothe a sore throat.** Mix two tablespoons French's Mustard, juice of half a lemon, one tablespoon salt, one tablespoon honey, and one-and-a-half cups boiling water. Cover and let cool for fifteen minutes, then gargle.

Invented
1904

The Name
In the fourteenth century, Dijon's mustard makers adopted Duke Philip the Bold's motto, *"Mout me tarde"* ("I ardently desire"). Legend holds that this motto was shortened to *moutarde*—the French name for the condiment. French's Mustard is not named for the country, but rather, after company founder Robert T. French.

A Short History

Around 3000 B.C.E., mustard was first cultivated and used in India and China. The Romans turned mustard into a paste by adding grape juice, vinegar, oil, and honey. The Romans are credited with having brought mustard to Gaul (modern-day France). In the thirteenth century, the Provost of Paris granted the vinegar makers of Dijon the right to make mustard, paving the way for Dijon to become the French capital of mustard. Around 1720, in Durham, England, a Mrs. Clements developed a process for extracting the husk from mustard seeds and milling a smooth mustard powder, going into full production in 1729. In nineteenth-century France, Maurice Grey introduced new equipment to speed up the production and developed Grey Poupon Mustard, keeping his mustard recipe in a safe. J. & J. Colman, founded in 1804 by Jeremiah Colman in Norwich, became synonymous with mustard in Britain.

In 1880, fifty-seven-year-old Robert T. French founded a spice company in the hopes of providing a livelihood for his three sons. By 1885 the company was operating out of an old flour mill in Rochester, New York, eventually manufacturing mustard. In 1904, the Frenches concocted a mild, bright-yellow mustard that quickly became a national favorite. In 1998, Reckitt & Colman, the company formed by the 1954 merger of Reckitt & Sons (a flour-milling business started by Isaac Reckitt in England in 1819) and mustard-maker J. & J. Colman, acquired the R. T. French Company.

Ingredients

Distilled vinegar, water, No. 1 grade mustard seed, salt, turmeric, paprika, spice, garlic powder, natural flavor

Strange Facts

■ Hippocrates, the Greek physician and philosopher, used mustard in poultices to treat bronchitis, pneumonia, and rheumatism.

■ Aesculapius, the Greek god of medicine and healing, was credited with having created mustard.

■ In the New Testament, Jesus compares the kingdom of God to a mustard seed (Mark 4).

■ Pliny the Elder (33–79 C.E.) outlined the medicinal uses of mustard in *Natural History*.

■ One of the earliest recipes for preparing mustard was published in the first century C.E. in *De Re Rustica* by Lucius Junius Moderatus, a retired Roman legionnaire.

■ Nicholas Culpeper (1616–1654), the famous seventeenth-century herbalist and physician, recommended the use of mustard in poultices for fevers, sciatica, and rheumatic pains.

■ King Louis XI of France (1423–1483) carried his own personal pot of mustard, made for him by a Dijon mustard maker, wherever he went.

■ Mustard has been used throughout history as a symbol of fertility because of the mustard plant's prolificacy.

■ In William Shakespeare's *As You Like It*, Touchstone says, "The mustard was good."

■ French's Mustard is 100-percent natural.

■ Colonel Mustard is a character in the board game Clue.

■ In the 1978 movie *National Lampoon's Animal House*, Bluto (played by John Belushi) pours an entire jar of mustard on himself during the toga party and smears it all over his shirt.

■ The Mount Horeb Mustard Museum in Mount Horeb, Wisconsin, houses the largest collection of mustards in the world, with over 2,000 different types of mustard. Subscribe to the museum's newsletter, *The Proper Mustard*, by calling 1-800-438-6878.

■ Colman's Mustard Shop and Museum in Bridewell Alley, Norwich, England, displays the history of mustard production and sells a selection of mustards, pots, and mustard paraphernalia emblazoned with the company name.

■ "Mean Mr. Mustard," a song by John Lennon and Paul McCartney, can be heard on the Beatles' *Abbey Road* album.

Distribution

■ French's Mustard is America's Favorite Mustard.

■ Reckitt & Colman also makes Frank's RedHot Sauce, French's Potato Sticks, French's Worcestershire Sauce, and French's French Fried Onions.

For More Information

■ Reckitt & Colman, Inc., 1655 Valley Road, P.O. Box 943, Wayne, NJ 07474-0945. Or telephone 1-800-841-1256.

■ Mount Horeb Mustard Museum, 109 East Main Street, P.O. Box 468, Mount Horeb, WI, 53572.

■ Colman's Mustard Shop and Museum, Bridewell Alley, Norwich, England.

Thirst Quencher

■ **Clean a toilet.** Pour two cups of Gatorade into the toilet bowl, let sit for one hour, then brush and flush clean. The citric acid in Gatorade removes stains from vitreous china.

■ **Relieve morning sickness.** Drinking Gatorade helps maintain the body's balance of electrolytes, which regulate the body's electrochemical balance.

■ **Combat the effects of diarrhea.** Drinking Gatorade replenishes the electrolytes and glucose being drained from your body during a bout with diarrhea.

■ **Relieve the pangs of food poisoning.** Drinking Gatorade replaces the electrolytes (particularly potassium and sodium) and fluids flushed out of your system by vomiting and diarrhea.

■ **Stave off heat exhaustion.** Dehydration or profuse sweating causes a rise in body temperature, resulting in loss of appetite, headache, dizziness, and sometimes nausea and vomiting. Drinking Gatorade replaces electrolytes (the potassium and salt lost through perspiration) and fluids.

■ **Settle your stomach after a bout of vomiting and prevent dehydration.** Drink Gatorade to replace the electrolytes and fluids flushed out by vomiting.

■ **Cure a hangover.** Since dehydration is the basic cause of a hangover, drinking Gatorade, which is absorbed into the body faster than water or fruit juice, quickly rehydrates the body, remedying the hangover.

■ **Store sugar.** A clean, empty, one-gallon Gatorade bottle makes an excellent container for storing sugar.

■ **Store birdseed or pet food.** Pour an open box or bag of birdseed or pet food into a clean, empty Gatorade bottle and secure the lid to keep the pet food fresh and free from insects and mice.

■ **Make a flower vase.** Empty and clean a Gatorade bottle, then remove the label. Fill halfway with water and fill with flowers.

■ **Make a megaphone.** Remove the cap and cut off the bottom of an empty, clean Gatorade bottle.

■ **Make a drill holster.** Cut off the bottom half of a clean, empty Gatorade bottle, on the diagonal. With screws, attach the back of the bottle to the wall above your workbench so the drill head fits through the mouth hole.

■ **Make a hot cap.** Cut off the bottom of an empty, clean Gatorade bottle and place the bottle over seedlings. Take the cap off during the day, and replace the cap at night.

■ **Make bowling pins.** Collect ten clean, empty Gatorade bottles, decorate, if you wish, with Con-Tact Paper, and use a rubber ball to bowl in the backyard.

Invented
1965

The Name
Gatorade is named after the Florida Gators, the football team at the University of Florida. The suffix -*ade* means "product"—usually used for sweet drinks like lemonade, limeade, and orangeade.

A Short History
A University of Florida nephrologist, Dr. Robert Cade, and a team of scientists concocted Gatorade in 1965 to sustain the school's football team—the Florida Gators. The new sports drink gave the Gators greater endurance in the second half of their games, resulting in a winning season. The Stokely–Van Camp Co. acquired the formula and turned the drink into a moneymaker, before being acquired by Quaker in 1983. Two years later, the Gatorade Company established the Gatorade Exercise Physiology Laboratory in Barrington, Illinois, to research exercise science, sports medicine, and the formulation of beverages and foods for physically active people worldwide.

Ingredients

Water, sucrose syrup, glucose-fructose syrup, citric acid, natural lemon and lime flavors with other natural flavors, salt, sodium citrate, monopotassium phosphate, ester gum, yellow 5

Strange Facts

■ Gatorade rehydrates the body 30 percent faster than water.

■ The higher the percentage of carbohydrate in a fluid, the slower that fluid is absorbed by the body. Gatorade Thirst Quencher, containing 6-percent carbohydrate, is rapidly absorbed by the body. Beverages containing more than 7-percent carbohydrate (such as fruit juices, soft drinks, and some sports drinks) are not recommended beverages during exercise.

■ The sodium and glucose in Gatorade (plus the taste of the beverage) stimulates people to drink more fluid voluntarily until the body is rehydrated.

■ The sodium in Gatorade helps people maintain body fluids. Water, caffeinated beverages, and alcoholic beverages activate urine production, causing people to lose fluids.

■ Consuming beverages that contain less than 7-percent carbohydrate during exercise enables a person to work out longer and harder and feel better. Carbohydrates provide the body with an easy-to-use energy source. Drinking 32 ounces of Gatorade Thirst Quencher (approximately 7 grams of carbohydrate) during each hour of exercise will spark an improvement in performance.

■ When you feel thirsty, you are already in the early stages of dehydration.

- Taste preferences differ during exercise than at rest. Gatorade is formulated to taste best when people are hot, sweaty, and thirsty.
- Drinking carbonated beverages during exercise increases the risk of nausea. The carbonation also makes it difficult to ingest fluids quickly.
- Chicago Bull Michael Jordan agreed to endorse Gatorade for ten years for a reported $18 million.
- Gatorade, according to *Time* magazine, "has become highly visible to sports fans, in the form of the ubiquitous large green-and-orange vats of the drink in dugouts or near team benches at major-league events. Hardly a postgame interview passes without a shot of the MVP taking a sip from a paper cup labeled 'Gatorade.'"
- Gatorade is the official sports drink of major league baseball, the National Football League, the National Basketball Association, NASCAR, and the Professional Golfers' Association.
- In 1987, the New York Giants doused coach Bill Parcells with a vat of Gatorade near the end of every winning game, inspiring other teams to mimic the ceremony.

Distribution

- Gatorade is available in sixteen flavors: Lemon-Lime, Orange, Fruit Punch, Citrus Cooler, Tropical Blast, Grape, Lemon-Ice, Cool Blue Raspberry, Wild Apple, Cherry Rush, Strawberry Kiwi, Mandarin Tangerine, Alpine Snow, Glacier Freeze, Whitewater Splash, and Riptide Rush.
- Gatorade, the bestselling sports drink, accounts for 80 percent of all sports drinks sold in the United States.

- In 1984, Gatorade sales were approximately $120 million. Ten years later, in 1998, Gatorade sales were more than $1.7 billion worldwide.
- Gatorade is sold on five continents around the world.

For More Information

The Gatorade Company, P.O. Box 049001, Chicago, IL 60604-9003. Or telephone 1-800-88-GATOR. On the Internet, visit www.gatorade.com.

Tires

■ **Make bumper guards in your garage.** Carefully cut wide strips from a used Goodyear Tire and nail them to the inside of your garage wall to align with your car's bumper.

■ **Make a doormat.** Using a hacksaw and a utility knife, carefully cut a used Goodyear Tire into short strips, and wire together.

■ **Prevent accidents on docks, ramps, and stairways.** Using a hacksaw, carefully cut flat strips of rubber from a used Goodyear Tire and nail or glue them to docks, ramps, and stairways.

■ **Make a wading pool.** Drape a clean shower curtain over a clean, used Goodyear Tire and fill with water.

■ **Prevent a boat from crashing into a dock.** Hang used Goodyear tires securely from the dock to protect the boat.

■ **Make sandals.** With a utility knife or table saw, carefully cut two flat sections from the tire, each approximately 6 by 12 inches. Using a piece of chalk, trace around the outside of each of your feet, leaving one inch extra around and adding wings at the toe and heel. Cut out the pattern, cut slits in the wings, thread leather straps through the slits, and hold the straps together with rivets.

Invented
1899

The Name
Goodyear is named after Charles Goodyear, the man who invented vulcanized rubber.

A Short History
In 1898, thirty-eight-year-old Frank Seiberling bought a converted strawboard factory at 1144 East Market Street on the banks of the Little Cuyahoga River in east Akron, Ohio, with a $3,500 down payment—using money he borrowed from his brother-in-law. Seiberling named his company after Charles Goodyear, a man he never knew, but who had, in 1839, invented the vulcanization process for rubber. With just thirteen employees, Seiberling began producing a line of bicycle and carriage tires, horseshoe pads, and poker chips.

In 1899, Goodyear introduced its first pneumatic tire for automobiles, followed by the tubeless tire in 1903 and the pneumatic truck tire in 1916, making Goodyear the largest tire manufacturer in the world. That same year, Goodyear established its own rubber plantations in Sumatra, and within ten years, Goodyear was the largest rubber company in the world.

Goodyear acquired rights to make zeppelins in 1924, and by the 1930s, Goodyear blimps were flying nationwide. The company opened its first stores in the 1930s, acquired Kelly-Springfield in 1935, and began producing synthetic rubber tires in 1937. During World War II, Goodyear, which had supplied airplane tires during World War I, made thousands of Corsair fighter planes, blimps, rubber aircraft parts, munitions, and tank tracks.

In 1947, Goodyear launched the first nylon-cord tire, followed in 1962 by the polyester-cord tire, the industry's primary reinforcing material. Although Michelin introduced the first radial tire in 1966, Goodyear introduced four lines of steel-belted radial tires and was selling more radial tires than any other tire maker by 1980.

Ingredients
Vulcanized rubber, steel belts

Strange Facts
■ Charles Goodyear, the man the company's name memorializes, died absolutely penniless despite his discovery of vulcanization after a long and courageous search that bordered on obsession.

- When Goodyear was founded, rubber and cotton had to be transported from halfway around the world to landlocked Akron, Ohio, a town that had only limited rail transportation.
- Goodyear founder Frank Seiberling chose the company's distinctive winged-foot trademark, inspired by a newel-post statuette of the Roman god Mercury in the Seiberling home.
- Although Goodyear got its start making bicycle tires, today the company makes tires for virtually every vehicle—except bicycles.
- Goodyear is often confused with B. F. Goodrich, Co., also of Akron, Ohio.
- In the 1977 movie *Black Sunday*, terrorists blow up the Goodyear Blimp over the Orange Bowl.
- Although the Goodyear Blimp is one of the world's most recognized corporate symbols, there are only three Goodyear Blimps in the United States—the *Eagle* in Los Angeles, the *Stars & Stripes* in Pompano Beach, Florida, and the *Spirit of Akron* in Akron, Ohio. The company also operates blimps in Europe, South America, and Australia.
- Goodyear Tires went to the moon in 1971 on the *Apollo 14* Lunar Rover.
- Aside from tires, Goodyear used to make shoe soles and heels, and at one time also made enriched uranium for nuclear reactors.
- As of 1999, Goodyear had more than 100,000 employees. That's nearly one-half the population of Akron, Ohio, the city where Goodyear was founded with thirteen employees.

Distribution
- In 1998, Goodyear's sales exceeded $13.1 billion (including over $11.2 billion worth of tires and related products).

For More Information

Goodyear, 1144 East Market Street, Akron, OH 44316. On the Internet, visit www.goodyear.com.

Irish Spring

Soap

■ **Repulse deer.** Drill a hole in a wrapped bar of Irish Spring Soap and, using string, hang it around crops. Deer mistake the smell of deodorant soap for humans, and flee.

■ **Freshen the air in your car.** Place a wrapped bar of Irish Spring Soap under the front seat.

■ **Lubricate zippers.** Rub the teeth of the zipper with a bar of Irish Spring Soap to make the zipper glide easier.

■ **Prevent campfire soot from sticking to the bottom of pots and pans.** Thinly coat the bottoms of pots and pans with Irish Spring Soap before putting them over an open fire.

■ **Prevent musty suitcases.** Place a wrapped bar of Irish Spring Soap inside empty luggage before storing.

■ **Deodorize shoes or sneakers.** Place a wrapped bar of

Irish Spring Soap in your shoes or sneakers overnight so they'll smell great in the morning.

■ **Stop insect bites from itching.** Apply wet Irish Spring Soap to the bite. When the soap dries, the skin will feel anesthetized.

■ **Lubricate furniture drawers and windows.** Rub Irish Spring Soap on the casters of drawers and windows so they slide open and shut easily.

■ **Eliminate odors in dirty laundry.** Place a wrapped bar of Irish Spring Soap at the bottom of a laundry bag or hamper.

■ **Make a pin cushion.** Using a wrapped bar of Irish Spring Soap as a pin cushion makes needles glide through fabric.

■ **Lubricate a handsaw blade.** Rub a bar of Irish Spring Soap across the sides and teeth of the saw to help the blade glide through wood.

■ **Fix small holes in walls.** Rub a bar of Irish Spring Soap over the hole until it looks flat and even, then paint.

■ **Lubricate nails and screws.** Nails and screws rubbed with Irish Spring Soap will go in easier.

■ **Freshen the air in your drawers or closets.** Place a wrapped bar of Irish Spring Soap in dresser drawers or the linen closet to keep them smelling fresh.

Invented

1972

The Name

The name "Irish Spring" suggests that washing with this deodorant soap will make you feel and smell like springtime in Ireland. The green box and green color of the soap evoke the green countryside of Ireland, also called "the Emerald Isle."

A Short History

In 1806, William Colgate, who came to America in 1795 from England, founded his starch, soap, and candle business on Dutch Street in New York City. In 1850, after moving his factory to Jersey City, Colgate produced a variety of soaps. By 1906, the company's line of products included many laundry soaps, 160 different kinds of toilet soap, and 625 varieties of perfume. In 1928, Colgate Company merged with Palmolive-Peet Company—created in 1926 when the Palmolive Company (founded in 1898 as the B. J. Johnson Soap Company) merged with the Peet Brothers (a soap company founded in Kansas City, Kansas, in 1872).

In 1953, six years after introducing Fab Detergent and Ajax Cleanser, the company changed its name to Colgate-Palmolive Company, then introduced Palmolive Dishwashing Liquid in 1966. Colgate Toothpaste was reformulated with MFP Fluoride (monofluorophosphate) in 1968. In 1972, the company introduced Irish Spring Deodorant Soap, which was reformulated in 1980, 1986, 1993, and 1996.

Ingredients

Soap (sodium tallowate, sodium cocate, and/or sodium palm kernelate types), water, stearic acid (skin conditioner), coconut and/or palm-kernel acid, glycerin (skin conditioner), fragrance, sodium chloride, titanium dioxide, pentasodium pentetate, BHT, D&C Green No. 8, FD&C Green No. 3

Strange Facts

■ Nearly 4,000 years ago, the Mesopotamians and Phoenicians used woodashes and water to clean themselves, and then applied oil to their bodies to prevent their skin from becoming irritated. Eventually, they made soap from ashes, various plants, and natural oils and animal fats.

■ Archaeologists excavated a fully equipped soap factory in the ruins of Pompeii, the Roman resort town destroyed by a volcano in 79 C.E.

■ Prior to the introduction of modern hygiene in the nineteenth century, the human body was often infected with parasites which caused the Black Death plague, typhus epidemics, cholera, and many other illnesses.

■ Body odor is not caused by perspiration, but rather by bacteria on the skin surface breaking down the perspiration. Left uncleansed, the skin becomes a breeding ground for germs.

■ The average American uses 30.5 pounds of soap and detergents every year.

■ There are more Irish people in New York City than in Dublin, Ireland.

Distribution

■ The Colgate-Palmolive Company also makes Colgate toothpastes, toothbrushes, mouth rinse and professional dental products, and brands including Mennen, Palmolive, Softsoap, Palmolive, Ajax, and Fab.

■ Colgate-Palmolive is a $9 billion consumer-products powerhouse, operates in over two hundred world markets, and approximately 70 percent of its sales comes from international operations.

■ Irish Spring is available in Original, Waterfall Clean, Sport, and Aloe.

For More Information

Colgate-Palmolive Company, 300 Park Avenue, New York, NY 10022. Or telephone 1-800-221-4607. On the Internet, visit www.colgate.com.

Marshmallows

■ **Decorate a Christmas tree.** String Jet-Puffed Marshmallows together with a needle and thread to form long chains, and drape them around the tree.

■ **Prevent an ice-cream sugar cone from dripping out the bottom.** Tuck a Jet-Puffed Marshmallow inside the sugar cone, then fill the cone with ice cream.

■ **Construct molecular models.** Use toothpicks and Jet-Puffed Marshmallows to construct models of molecular structures, or simply for the pleasure of building something.

■ **Play the marshmallow kissing game.** Using a sewing needle, string a Jet-Puffed Marshmallow in the middle of a four-foot-long piece of thread. Have each party guest choose a partner of the opposite sex. Each partner takes one end of the thread, places it in their mouth, and then tries to wind the thread around their tongue until they reach the marshmallow. The first team to eat the marshmallow wins. Of course, the first team to get to the marshmallow winds up kissing.

■ **Make s'mores.** Roast two Jet-Puffed Marshmallows over a campfire, place the roasted marshmallows and a piece of a Hershey's Chocolate Bar between two graham crackers like a sandwich, allowing the heat from the marshmallows to melt the chocolate. S'mores get their name from the fact that once you've eaten one of these treats, you usually want "some more."

■ **Retrieve a coin or piece of jewelry that has fallen down a drain.** Tie a fishing weight to a long string, stretch out a Jet-Puffed Marshmallow repeatedly until it is a sticky wad, attach it to the bottom of the weight, dangle it down the drain, let it take hold, then pull up.

■ **Make cupcake frosting.** Two minutes before removing a pan of cupcakes from the oven, top each cupcake with a Jet-Puffed Marshmallow. It will melt into a delicious frosting.

■ **Stack marshmallows.** For fun, see who can stack the most Jet-Puffed Marshmallows vertically on a tabletop.

■ **Play marshmallow toss.** Line up six beach pails in a vertical row and place a piece of

masking tape two feet in front of the first pail. Standing behind the line of masking tape, toss a Jet-Puffed Marshmallow into each bucket, beginning with the closest one. The first person to toss a marshmallow into the farthest bucket wins.

■ **Run the marshmallow obstacle course.** Have contestants run an obstacle course while balancing marshmallows on two spoons—one in each hand. Whoever drops a marshmallow must start at the beginning again.

■ **Play "marshmallow golf."** Try putting using a Jet-Puffed Marshmallow as the ball. Use coffee mugs for the holes. The player with the fewest strokes wins.

Invented

1953

The Name

The name "Jet-Puffed" was coined to describe a special new manufacturing process which infused air into the marshmallow, giving it a light, fluffy texture. Marshmallows were originally made by sweetening, whipping, and molding the gummy sap from the root of the marshmallow, a pink-flowered European perennial herb *(Althaea officinalis)*.

A Short History

The pharaohs of ancient Egypt discovered that part of the mallow plant grown in marshes could be made into a delicious confection—reserved for royalty only. In the nineteenth century, French candy makers, unable to keep up with the demand for marshmallows, devised the "starch mogul" system—making marshmallows in cornstarch molds and replacing mallow root with gelatin. In 1948, marshmallow maker Alex Doumak invented the "extrusion process"—a means of piping the fluffy marshmallow mixture—a combination of corn syrup, sugar, albumen, and gelatin—through long tubes and cutting its tubular shape into equal pieces.

Kraft Foods, Inc. introduced Jet-Puffed Marshmallows in the early 1953, and two years later, Favorite Brands International bought the Jet-Puffed Marshmallow business from Kraft.

Ingredients

Corn syrup, sugar, dextrose, food starch–modified (corn), water, gelatin, tetrasodium pyrophosphate, artificial and natural flavor, artificial colors (contains Blue 1)

Strange Facts

■ Marshmallows do not contain any marshmallow.

■ The Stay-Puft Marshmallow Man—who came to life in the motion picture *Ghostbusters* starring Bill Murray, Dan Aykroyd, Harold Ramis, and Sigourney Weaver—was a fictional trademark character created especially for the movie. The name "Stay-Puft" was a takeoff on Jet-Puffed Marshmallows, and the fluffy marshmallow character is a hybrid of Campy, the spokesmarshmallow for Campfire Marshmallows and the Michelin Tire Man.

■ Freezing marshmallows prevents them from going stale.

■ While running for the Republican presidential nomination in the 1980 New Hampshire primary, George Bush called President Jimmy Carter a "little marshmallow."

■ More than 50 million bags of Jet-Puffed Marshmallows are sold each year. If laid end-to-end, they would stretch from New York City to Los Angeles three times.

■ The Ligonier Marshmallow Festival, the world's only marshmallow festival, is held annually over Labor Day weekend in Noble County, Indiana, attracting more than 20,000 marshmallow lovers who roast, toast, cook with, eat, and have fun with marshmallows.

Distribution

■ Jet-Puffed Marshmallows, the bestselling marshmallow in the United States, are available in Regular and Miniature sizes, and a variety of colors and shapes, including Boo-mallows, Holiday-mallows, Bunny-mallows, and Star-mallows.

■ More Jet-Puffed Miniature Marshmallows are sold each year than the traditional big ones—representing 54.1 percent of sales.

For More Information

Favorite Brands International, 2121 Waukegan, Dept. CRL, Bannockburn, IL 60015. Or telephone 1-800-244-4596. On the Internet, visit www.jetpuffed.com.

Kodak

Film

■ **Carry salt, pepper, and other condiments while camping.** Kodak Film canisters make excellent storage canisters for carrying spices while camping and picnicking.

■ **Pack a sewing kit.** Place a couple of needles, some thread, buttons, and safety pins in a Kodak Film canister.

■ **Hold stamps.** Keep a roll of stamps in a Kodak Film canister.

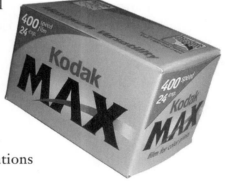

■ **Keep pills separate while traveling.** Label an assortment of Kodak Film canisters to carry aspirin or other pills and medications while traveling.

■ **Store small nails, screws, nuts, or bolts.** Use a Kodak Film canister.

■ **Hold coins.** Kodak Film canisters make excellent storage containers for quarters, dimes, nickels. Keep a canister filled with change in the car so you always have change for parking meters, tolls, vending machines, washing machines, pay phones, and showers.

■ **Store emergency matches while camping or back-packing.** A Kodak Film canister makes a superb place to keep matches.

■ **Store jewelry.** Keep earrings, rings, and necklaces each in their own individual Kodak Film canister for safekeeping.

■ **Carry earplugs.** Keep your earplugs for swimming or sleeping in a Kodak Film canister.

■ **Organize your desk drawer.** Keep paper clips and rubber bands in a Kodak Film canister.

■ **Store money while camping or boating.** Keep your money rolled up in a Kodak Film canister.

Invented
1891

The Name
Photography pioneer George Eastman coined the meaning-less word *Kodak* himself. "I chose that name," Eastman said, "because I knew a trade name must be short, vigorous, incapable of being misspelled to an extent that will destroy its identity, and, in order to satisfy trademark laws, it must mean nothing. The letter *k* had been a favorite with me—it seemed a strong, incisive sort of letter. Therefore, the word I wanted had to start with *k*. Then it became a question of trying out a great number of combinations of letters that made words starting and ending with *k*. The word *Kodak* is the result."

A Short History

In the 1870s, George Eastman, a junior bank clerk in Rochester, New York, took up photography as a hobby and began experimenting with emulsions for dry-coating glass plates to simplify the picture-taking process. Realizing the profit to be made selling dry plates to commercial photographers, Eastman began cooking up various emulsions in his mother's kitchen at night. In 1880, using his own savings to lease office space, he went into business manufacturing dry plates. Eastman then devised a way to replace cumbersome glass plates with emulsion-coated paper film. When professional photographers failed to switch to the new film, Eastman decided to make it available to the general public.

In 1888, George Eastman introduced the Kodak—a small box camera loaded with a roll of stripping paper for a hundred exposures. After taking pictures, the customer would send the camera to Rochester where the Eastman Kodak Company would develop and print the photographs and reload the camera with a new roll of stripping paper. The following year, Kodak introduced transparent film. In 1891, Eastman made rolls of transparent film, spooled into metal canisters, available for sale to the public, revolutionizing photography.

Ingredients

Celluloid, dry emulsion

Strange Facts

■ George Eastman dropped out of school at age fourteen to help support his widowed mother and two sisters, one of whom was crippled by polio.

■ While trying to devise a name for his new camera, George Eastman searched the dictionary for inspiration. Today, the dictionary contains the word he coined.

■ The flexible, transparent film invented by George Eastman in 1889 prompted Thomas Edison to invent the movie camera and projector—giving birth to the motion-picture industry.

■ Oddly, very few photographs of George Eastman were taken.

■ George Eastman modestly donated $20 million to the Massachusetts Institute of Technology as "Mr. Smith." The mysterious "Mr. Smith" was immortalized in a MIT song.

Distribution

■ Kodak films are available worldwide.

For More Information

Eastman-Kodak, Rochester, NY 14650. Or telephone 1-800-242-2424. On the Internet, visit www.kodak.com.

Chocolate Candies

■ **Go fishing.** M&M's Chocolate Candies make excellent bait for catching mullet, bass, and shad.

■ **Teach kids how to sort colors.** Give children a bag of M&M's Chocolate Candies and have them sort the M&M's by color.

■ **Teach kids how to count.** *The M&M's Brand Chocolate Candies Counting Book* by Barbara Barbieri McGrath uses M&M's to teach young readers to count up to ten, using the lovable M&M's characters and the new blue M&M's.

■ **Bake with M&M's Chocolate Candies.** Aside from decorating ice-cream sundaes, cookies, cakes, and brownies, you can make dozens of delicious dishes with M&M's Chocolate Mini Baking Bits (a third the size of regular M&M's Chocolate Candies). M&M/Mars offers recipes for dozens of desserts, including Marbled Biscotti, M&M's Cookies, Double-Decker Confetti Brownies, Chocolate Marbled Blondies, Marbled Mocha Drops, and Giant Pizzazz Cookie.

Invented
1941

The Name
M&M's are the combined initials of company founder Forrest E. Mars and his former associate Bruce Murrie.

A Short History
After his graduation from Yale University, Forrest Mars went to work for his father, Frank Mars, the inventor of the Snickers Bar and the Milky Way Bar. After several disagreements, Forrest moved to England and started his own Mars candy company in the 1930s, also making pet food. During World War II, Forrest returned home with the rights to market British Smarties in the United States—as M&M's. In 1941, he formed a company in Newark, New Jersey, to make the candies. In 1954, Mars introduced M&M's Peanut Chocolate Candies (which only came in brown and were sold in a paper tube for 5 cents) and the advertising slogan, "The milk chocolate melts in your mouth . . . not in your hand." Six years later, Mars introduced red, yellow, orange, and green M&M's Peanut Chocolate Candies. Forrest Mars took over

the company when his father died, and in 1973, he turned over the reins of the family-run business to his two sons, Forrest Jr. and John.

Ingredients

Milk chocolate (sugar, chocolate, milk, cocoa butter, lactose, soy lecithin, salt, artificial flavors), sugar, cornstarch, and less than 1 percent of the following: corn syrup, gum acacia, coloring (includes Red 40 Lake, Blue 2 Lake, Yellow 5, Yellow 6, Blue 1 Lake, Red 40, Blue 1), dextrin

Strange Facts

■ The Mayan and Aztec civilizations of Central America used to make a drink from the beans of the cacao tree. In 1544, Dominican friars brought the drink back to Europe. Three hundred years later, a method was found to produce solid chocolate.

■ To make M&M's Chocolate Candies, chocolate is poured into tiny molds to create the chocolate centers. After they harden, the chocolates are rotated in large containers as several coatings of liquid candy are sprayed onto them. The single-colored batches of red, yellow, blue, green, brown, and orange candy are mixed together and then sifted to eliminate misshapen pieces. A conveyor belt carries each piece in its own little indentation past rubber etch rollers that gently touch each candy, printing that distinctive *m* on its shell. A packaging machine then weighs the M&M's, pours the proper amount into each bag, and heat-seals each package. The entire processing time required to make one M&M's Chocolate Candy is approximately twelve hours.

■ The average bag of M&M's Plain Chocolate Candies contains 30 percent browns, 20 percent each of yellows and reds, and 10 percent each of oranges, greens, and blues. The average bag of M&M's Peanut Chocolate Candies contains 20 percent each of browns, yellows, reds, and blues, and 10 percent each of greens and oranges.

■ In 1941, Mars introduced brown, yellow, orange, red, green, and violet M&M's. Violet M&M's were replaced in 1950 by tan M&M's.

■ During World War II, M&M's were part of soldiers' C rations and were also eaten by U.S. soldiers in the Gulf War.

■ The *m*'s were not printed on M&M's until 1950. Originally printed in black, the *m*'s were changed to white in 1954.

■ In 1976, scientists determined that Red Dye No. 2 caused cancer in rats. To alleviate any fears, M&M's Chocolate Candies stopped making red M&M's (which did not even contain Red Dye No. 2), sparking protests from the Society for the Restoration and Preservation of Red M&M's. In 1987, the company brought back red M&M's, using FD&C Red No. 40, as produced before.

■ In 1982, M&M's rocketed into space aboard the first space shuttle.

■ M&M's are on permanent display as part of the space food exhibit at the National Air and Space Museum of the Smithsonian Institute in Washington, D.C.

■ In the movie *Peggy Sue Got Married*, Peggy Sue goes back in time to the 1950s, where she sees her younger sister eating M&M's Chocolate Candies and exclaims, "Don't eat the red ones." Ironically, there was never any problem with red M&M's.

■ In 1995, after more than 10 million consumers voted for their favorite color M&M's, tan M&M's were replaced with blue M&M's.

■ When Steven Spielberg made the motion picture *E.T.*, he asked M&M/Mars for permission to use M&M's in the scene where Elliot first befriends the extraterrestrial. M&M/Mars turned down the opportunity. Spielberg used Reese's Pieces instead, causing sales of the rival Chocolate Candies to skyrocket.

■ When astronaut Shannon Lucid returned to Earth in September 1996 from Russia's space station *Mir* after 188 days in space (more time in weightlessness than any American or woman in the world), NASA administrator Dan Goldin presented her with a gift from President Bill Clinton: a nineteen-pound box of red, white, and blue M&M's wrapped in golden foil and embossed with the presidential seal. Lucid had said she craved M&M's while aboard *Mir*.

■ M&M's Colorworks™, a unique dispenser system, blends twenty-one brilliantly colored M&M's Plain Chocolate Candies in any combination imaginable. The colors include white, gold, dark blue, dark green, light purple, maroon, black, light blue, teal green, purple, dark pink, gray, pink, aqua green, and cream plus the original colors of red, green, yellow, brown, orange, and blue. M&M's Colorworks™ are available at selected candy stores or through www.m-ms.com.

■ On the television talk show *Politically Incorrect with Bill Maher*, renowned attorney Alan Dershowitz, who was raised as an observant Orthodox Jew, admitted that as a child he never ate M&M's because, at that time, the candies were not kosher. Today, M&M's Chocolate Candies are kosher.

■ Green M&M's are considered to be an aphrodisiac. At wedding showers, guests often present the future bride with a bag of M&M's with all the green candies carefully removed and placed in a second bag specifically reserved for the wedding night. An M&M/Mars brochure states: "Although many consumers ask us about the special qualities of green M&M's Chocolate Candies, we cannot explain any extraordinary 'powers' attributed to this color, either scientifically or medically."

Distribution

■ The M&M's brand is the number one candy brand in the world.

■ More than 300 million individual M&M's Chocolate Candies are made every day. That's more than 124 billion M&M's each year.

■ If laid side by side, the number of M&M's produced each year would reach to the moon and back more than five times.

■ Mars, Inc., is one of the largest private companies in the United States.

■ Besides M&M's Chocolate Candies, Mars makes Combos Snacks, Dove Bars, Kudos, Mars, Milky Way, Skittles, Snickers, Starburst, 3 Musketeers, and Twix. The company also makes Kal Kan Pet Food, Uncle Ben's Rice, and electronic products.

For More Information

M&M/Mars, Consumer Affairs, 800 High Street, Hackettstown, NJ 07840. Or telephone 1-800-627-7852. On the Internet, visit www.m-ms.com.

Mrs. Stewart's

Liquid Bluing

■ **Whiten white pets.** Pet owners use Mrs. Stewart's Liquid Bluing to whiten white pet fur—from a poodle being groomed for a show to a palomino's tail being readied for a parade. Just add a couple of drops of Mrs. Stewart's Liquid Bluing in the rinse water.

■ **Make a Magic Salt Crystal Garden.** With a hammer, break up five charcoal briquets into one inch chunks. Place the pieces in the bottom of a two-quart glass bowl. In a clean, empty jar, mix six tablespoons salt, six tablespoons Mrs. Stewart's Liquid Bluing, one tablespoon ammonia, and two table-spoons water. Pour the mix-ture over the charcoal in the bowl. Sprinkle a few drops of food coloring over each piece of char-coal. Let the bowl sit undisturbed in a safe place for seventy-two hours. Fluffy, fragile crystals will form on top of the charcoal and some will climb up the sides of the bowl. The salt recrystallizes into beautiful, delicate coral-like formations. As the ammonia speeds up the evaporation of the water, the blue ion particles in the bluing, and the salt, get carried up into the porous charcoal, where the salt crystallizes around the blue particles as nuclei. These crystals are porous like a sponge, and the liquid below continues to move into the openings and evaporate, leaving layers of crystals. To keep the crystals growing, add another batch of ammonia, salt, bluing, and water.

■ **Whiten a lace tablecloth.** Mix a few drops of Mrs. Stewart's Liquid Bluing in a quart or more of water. Add the mixture to wash water or final rinse (water should appear light sky-blue).

■ **Give the water in a swimming pool an inviting blue appearance.** For standard pools (20 by 40 feet), add one or two bottles of Mrs. Stewart's Liquid Bluing where water is recirculated from the filter, being careful not to splash directly on pool surface. Do not use in aerated pools such as jacuzzis or whirlpools, as spotting can occur.

■ **Entice kids to take a bath.** Add a few drops of Mrs. Stewart's Liquid Bluing in the bathwater to get kids into the tub.

■ **Whiten white hair.** Adding a couple of drops of Mrs. Stewart's Liquid Bluing to the rinse water when washing gray or white hair eliminates yellowing and gives hair a lush whiteness that products made especially for that purpose cannot achieve. Mrs. Stewart's Liquid Bluing is perfectly safe, and a few drops cost less than a penny.

■ **Relieve the pain of insect bites.** In a booklet on treating snake and insect bites, the University of Arizona recommends using Mrs. Stewart's Liquid Bluing to treat the bite of a red harvester ant. The company has also received countless letters over the years reporting that a dab of Mrs. Stewart's Liquid Bluing immediately relieves a bee sting.

■ **Clean crystal.** A few drops of Mrs. Stewart's Liquid Bluing in the rinse water makes fine crystal and crystal chandeliers sparkle. Dust particles are purportedly repelled by the bluing so the crystal stays clean longer.

■ **Clean windows and mirrors.** A few drops of Mrs. Stewart's Liquid Bluing in a bucket of water makes mirrors and windows sparkle.

■ **Brighten the water in fountains, bird baths, and fish ponds.** A few drops of Mrs. Stewart's Liquid Bluing gives water a blue tinge without affecting the clarity of the water. Reportedly, adding bluing to birdbaths and fishponds also helps reduce algae buildup.

■ **Color a podiatric cast.** Add a few drops of Mrs. Stewart's Liquid Bluing to color the casting material used in podiatric laboratories. Tinting certain layers of plaster makes it easier to determine where to add more plaster or cut away excess plaster.

■ **Make sculpting easier.** Add a few drops of Mrs. Stewart's Bluing when mixing plaster of paris. Adding a blue color to certain layers of plaster makes it easier to determine where to add more plaster.

■ Glaze pottery with ease. Since glaze dries clear on wet clay (making it virtually impossible to know exactly which area was glazed), adding a few drops of Mrs. Stewart's Liquid Bluing to the glaze makes it easier to see which areas of the pottery have been painted with glaze. When the pottery is fired, the blue is burned away, leaving a beautiful clear glaze.

■ Detect leaks in drain systems, automotive cooling systems, and toilet tanks. Add a few drops of Mrs. Stewart's Liquid Bluing into a drain to locate a leak in the pipes, into an automobile coolant tank to find the source of a leak in the coolant system, or into a toilet holding tank to determine whether the tank leaks into the bowl, which wastes water.

■ Reduce the algae growth in garden lily ponds, fishponds, and feeding troughs of farm animals. Simply add a few drops of Mrs. Stewart's Liquid Bluing. Mrs. Stewart's Liquid Bluing contains a non-toxic amount of a pH balancer and a biocide to prevent the buildup of algae and bacteria.

■ Diminish reported cases of distemper in small farm animals. Add a few drops of Mrs. Stewart's Liquid Bluing to the drinking water of small farm animals. The biocide in Mrs. Stewart's Liquid Bluing prevents the build-up of algae and bacteria.

■ Color wallpaper paste to aid in even spreading. Mix a few drops of Mrs. Stewart's Liquid Bluing to the wallpaper paste so you can see how well you're covering the wallpaper.

■ **Re-blue denim jeans that have faded.** Simply use more Mrs. Stewart's Liquid Bluing than directed.

■ **Tie-dye T-shirts without chemicals.** In a bucket, mix one tablespoon Mrs. Stewart's Liquid Bluing in one gallon of water. Wrap rubber bands around sections of a white T-shirt, then submerge the T-shirt into the mixture in the bucket, wring well, let dry, then remove the rubberbands.

■**Color flowers.** Freshly cut carnations placed in a vase with a high content of Mrs. Stewart's Liquid Bluing in the water will by osmosis carry the blue color into the tips of the petals quickly.

Invented
1883

The Name
At the turn of the century, Alan Stewart acquired the right to the formula for this bluing product and decided to rename it after his wife. When she refused to let him use her photograph on the bottles, Stewart used a photograph of his mother-in-law.

A Short History
Color experts have distinguished approximately 300 shades of white—from pink-white to gray-white. The brightest whites have a slight bluish hue. In its original state, white cotton fabric and white raw wool is yellowish. Most of the

synthetic fibers are a grayish off-white. All these fabrics are bleached, usually by a chemical treatment, to remove the yellow color. Manufacturers then blue them, making them look snow-white. Eventually the bleach and the bluing agent wash out—returning the white fabrics to their original color. Adding a little diluted bluing to the rinse cycle gives white fabrics this blue hue again.

Mrs. Stewart's Liquid Bluing, a very fine blue iron powder suspended in water, optically whitens white fabric. It does not remove stains or clean, but merely adds a microscopic blue particle to white fabric that makes it appear whiter. Mrs. Stewart's Liquid Bluing is non-toxic, biodegradable, non-hazardous, and environmentally friendly.

Ingredients

Very fine blue iron powder [$Fe_2Fe_3(CN)_6$] suspended in water (a "colloidal suspension"), a non-toxic amount of a pH balancer, and a biocide (to prevent the buildup of algae and bacteria)

Strange Facts

■ Both a brand-new white shirt and a white shirt that has been laundered for a year appear white; but when the two shirts are placed next to each other, the blue hue in the new shirt becomes evident.

■ When two pieces of white fabric are placed under a spectrograph, the one with blue added will reflect more light, making the fabric appear its whitest.

■ To use Mrs. Stewart's Liquid Bluing in the wash cycle for your laundry, put one-quarter teaspoon of Mrs. Stewart's

Liquid Bluing into an empty, gallon plastic container, fill with cold water, shake well, then pour into the machine with clothes present. To use in the rinse cycle, mix less than one-eighth of a teaspoon of Mrs. Stewart's Liquid Bluing into an empty gallon plastic container, fill with cold water, shake well, then pour into the machine with clothes present.

■ In the early and middle 1900s, bluing was used by everyone who wanted white wash, and could be found in virtually all laundries. When washing was done by hand or in wringer washers, the second rinse tub was the bluing rinse. To capitalize on this trend, manufacturers began coloring their detergents and other additives blue. Many claimed that their products contained bluing.

■ A doctor doing research on skin cancer found that by boiling Mrs. Stewart's Liquid Bluing he could get a higher concentration of bluing to mark tissue samples for chemo-surgery. Bradley Products, Inc., the sister company to Mrs. Stewart's Liquid Bluing, now makes the Davidson Marking System, which includes a bluing-based dye in a set of five different colors of tissue dyes, with a sixth color available. Drug-testing companies also use Mrs. Stewart's Liquid Bluing in their procedures.

■ A liquid-fertilizer manufacturer added Mrs. Stewart's Liquid Bluing to his product in research experiments to follow the fertilizer through the plant and determine the rate of absorption.

■ If you accidently spill Mrs. Stewart's Liquid Bluing on fabric or use more bluing in your wash than directed, put the clothing in a five-gallon bucket with a tight lid (or in a plastic bag with a twist tie). Add a solution of two cups ammonia to one gallon cold water. Seal tightly to keep the fumes in. Let soak for twenty-four hours. Then run the clothing through a regular wash cycle with detergent only. Do not use bleach. Bleach will cause the bluing to set in permanently.

■ Some pool manufacturers and dealers who use Mrs. Stewart's Liquid Bluing in their display pools claim it helps close a sale.

■ All solids have an orderly pattern of atoms, which is repeated again and again. This orderly pattern, called "crystallinity," can be seen in a Magic Crystal Garden because the simple crystals reveal their particular atomic structure to the naked eye.

■ Crystal Gardens became popular during the Depression and are still known as a "Depression Flower" or "Coal Garden."

■ Because blue-white is the most intense white, most artists, when portraying a snow scene, will use a blue color to intensify the whiteness.

Distribution

■ Since 1883, Mrs. Stewart's Liquid Bluing has been the most effective, economical, and environmentally safe laundry whitener available.

For More Information

Luther Ford & Company, P.O. Box 201405, Bloomington, MN 55420. Or telephone 1-800-325-7785. On the Internet, visit www.mrsstewart.com.

■ Cure eczema. Rub a dab of Noxzema into the dry skin.

■ Remove makeup. Rub a dab of Noxzema over your face, then wash clean with water.

■ Lubricate pipe joints. Noxzema works as an oil lubricant for fitting pipe joints together.

■ Enjoy a massage. Noxzema is an excellent massage cream.

■ Remove scuff marks from patent-leather shoes. Apply Noxzema to a soft cloth and rub into the patent leather.

■ Take a soothing bath. Add two tablespoons of Noxzema to a warm bath as a bath oil.

■ Clean oil-based paint from hands. Noxzema removes paint and stains from hands more gently than turpentine.

■ Relieve itching from insect bites. Applying Noxzema over the affected areas alleviates itching.

■ **Remove chewing gum from hair or carpeting.** Rub a dollop of Noxzema into the bubble gum.

■ **Soften fingernails.** Warm Noxzema and use as a hot oil treatment to soften nails.

■ **Clean grease, ink, and oil from skin.** Rub Noxzema into the skin and wash clean with water.

■ **Pry apart two bowls or glasses.** Dribble a few drops of Noxzema down the sides, then slip the bowls or glasses apart.

■ **Polish wood furniture.** Apply a dab of Noxzema and buff clean.

■ **Remove dried glue and gum left from price tags and labels from glass and metal.** Apply Noxzema and wipe clean.

■ **Soothe sunburn.** Gently apply Noxzema to skin to soothe the sunburned area.

■ **Soften rough skin.** Apply Noxzema to rough skin on feet and elbows to help soften.

■ **Shave.** In a pinch, you can use Noxzema as shaving cream.

Invented

1914

The Name

A customer told Dr. George Bunting, "Your sunburn cream sure knocked my eczema," inspiring Bunting to change the name of Dr. Bunting's Sunburn Remedy to Noxzema—a clever combination of the misspelled word *knocks* and the last two syllables of the word *eczema*.

A Short History

In 1914, pharmacist Dr. George Bunting combined medication and vanishing cream in the prescription room of his Baltimore drugstore at 6 West North Avenue to create Dr. Bunting's Sunburn Remedy. He mixed, heated, and poured the skin cream into little blue jars from a huge coffeepot. When other druggists began ordering his sunburn remedy for their customers, Bunting decided to devote all his energies to marketing the skin cream—changing the name to Noxzema.

In 1917, the Noxzema Chemical Company was founded with sales of $5,214 and four employees. Three years later, Bunting opened the first Noxzema "factory" in a tiny house at 102 Lafayette Avenue in Baltimore. Bunting's fellow druggists helped finance the Noxzema company by placing Noxzema in their stores and buying shares of stock in the company—usually for $100 or less.

By 1925, sales reached $100,000, and Bunting launched Noxzema nationally, starting with New York City in 1926, followed by Chicago and the Midwest in 1928, the South and the Pacific Coast in 1930, and the Prairie and Rocky Mountain states in 1938. With national distribution in place, Noxzema began advertising on national radio broadcasts of *Professor*

Quiz. Sales jumped 40 percent in one season, and Noxzema began expanding into shaving cream, suntan lotions, and cold cream.

In 1938, sales reached $1 million. By 1944, sales had skyrocketed to $3 million. With a new factory completed in 1949, Noxzema improved production, and in 1961, the company launched Cover Girl. In 1966, Noxzema Chemical Company adopted the name Noxell Corporation. In 1989, Procter & Gamble Cosmetics and Fragrances bought Noxell. In 1999, they launched Noxzema Skin Fitness.

Ingredients

Water, stearic acid, linseed oil, soybean oil, fragrance, ammonium hydroxide, camphor, menthol, eucalyptus oil, propylene glycol, gelatin, calcium hydroxide

Strange Facts

■ Noxzema inventor George Bunting worked as a school principal for six years before pursuing a career as a pharmacist by enrolling in the University of Maryland's pharmacy school.

■ The little blue jars which Dr. Bunting once filled from a coffeepot are now filled by a machine at the rate of 120 jars per minute.

■ During Dr. Bunting's early attempts at financing Noxzema, he was on the verge of bankruptcy several times between 1914 and 1923—the first year he showed a small profit.

■ During World War II, the Noxzema Chemical Company manufactured over 63.2 million jars of Noxzema for GIs.

Distribution

■ Noxzema is sold in over one hundred countries and is produced in nine overseas locations.

■ Besides the original Noxzema Skin Cream, Noxzema makes shaving cream, cold cream, Cover Girl makeup, Cover Girl lipstick, and Noxzema Skin Fitness.

For More Information

Procter & Gamble Cosmetics and Fragrances, P.O. Box 599, Cincinnnati, OH 45201. Or telephone 1-800-436-4361. On the Internet, visit www.pg.com.

Ammonia

■ **Clean diamonds, rubies, and sapphires.** Mix equal parts Parsons' Ammonia and warm water, and drop the jewelry in for ten minutes. Rub gently with an old, soft, clean toothbrush. Let air-dry. **Do not use this formula for cleaning opals, pearls, turquoise, or coral.**

■ **Clean gold jewelry.** Soak jewelry in equal parts Parsons' Ammonia and lukewarm water for ten minutes, rub with a soft brush, and let dry without rinsing.

■ **Clean an oven.** Warm the oven, turn it off, then set one cup of Parsons' Ammonia inside the oven, and close overnight. In the morning, open all the kitchen windows, stand back, open the oven, and let it air out for one hour. Wash the oven walls and floor with soap and water, and wipe clean. **Only use this hint in kitchens with adequate ventilation.**

■ **Remove oil and grease stains from driveways and cement.** Add one-half to a full cup Parsons' Ammonia to one gallon warm water and apply to the surface. Brush or scrub, then hose clean.

■ **Make flowers bloom in winter.** Prune some twigs or branches of forsythia, crab apple, hawthorn, lilac, or other flowering trees and shrubs. Put the stems in a bucket of warm water, then drop in a cotton ball soaked with Parsons'

Ammonia. Put the pail and branches in a plastic bag and seal securely with a twist tie. The ammonia fumes will force blooms on the branches.

■ **Fertilize ferns.** Water the plant with a mixture of two tablespoons Parsons' Ammonia and one quart water to enrich the nitrogen content of the soil.

■ **Deodorize cat-urine stains.** Blot up the puddle, rub with a solution of vinegar and warm sudsy water, and let dry. Then rub the spot with a cloth dampened in Parsons' Ammonia, both deodorizing the spot and preventing the cat from urinating in that spot again. (Be sure to test the ammonia on an inconspicuous spot first to make sure it doesn't affect the color of the carpet.)

■ **Remove crayon marks from painted walls.** Scrub with a cloth soaked in Parsons' Ammonia.

■ **Clean carpets and upholstery.** Add two cups Parsons' Ammonia per gallon of warm water. (Be sure to test the ammonia on an inconspicuous spot first to make sure it doesn't affect the color.)

■ **Remove absorbed body oils from sheets, towels, and clothes.** Add one cup Parsons' Ammonia to the usual amount of granular detergent and launder as usual. **Never mix ammonia with chlorine bleach. Deadly fumes may form.**

■ **Clean pots, pan, and stove parts without scrubbing.** Put the removable parts (like the oven racks and the chrome rings on electric range ovens) in a plastic garbage bag, pour in two cups of Parsons' Ammonia, tie the bag securely shut, and leave it outside for several hours. Then rinse clean with the garden hose. **Do not use ammonia to clean aluminum pots, pans, or stove parts.**

■ **Remove ring-around-the-collar.** Mix one tablespoon Parsons' Ammonia, one-half teaspoon Tide, and one cup warm water. Rub the solution into the collar, let sit for thirty minutes, then launder as usual.

■ **Remove a cork from inside an empty wine bottle.** Pour Parsons' Ammonia into the bottle to cover the cork, and set aside in a well-ventilated spot. The cork will disintegrate in a few days.

■ **Polish silverware.** Mix equal parts Parsons' Ammonia with silver paste polish, apply with a soft cloth, and rinse clean.

■ **Loosen a tight screw or a rusted bolt.** Soak the screw or bolt with Parsons' Ammonia.

■ **Eliminate paint odor.** Fill a large pan with water, add one tablespoon Parsons' Ammonia, and place in the freshly painted room overnight.

■ **Remove wax from a linoleum or tile floor.** Mix one cup Parsons' Ammonia in one gallon water. Mop the floor, wait a few minutes, then wipe clean with clean rags. Be sure to clean small areas at a time to prevent the mixture from drying on the floor.

■ **Clean hairbrushes and combs.** Add three tablespoons Parsons' Ammonia to one quart warm water. Soak the hairbrushes and combs in the solution. Rinse and let dry.

■ **Clean narrow-necked bottles.** Fill the bottle with equal parts Parsons' Ammonia and water, add a handful of uncooked rice, and swirl to scour.

■ **Clean windows and mirrors.** Add four to eight tablespoons of Parsons' Ammonia to one quart warm water. Apply with a sponge, clean cloth, or pump spray bottle, and wipe dry.

■ **Keep crystal shining.** Wash crystal in a sink full of warm water and one-quarter cup of Parsons' Ammonia.

■ **Remove tarnish from brass.** Scrub brass lightly with a soft brush dampened with a little Parsons' Ammonia.

■ **Clean stains from stainless steel.** Rub the stainless steel with a cloth dampened with Parsons' Ammonia.

■ **Polish chrome.** Mix one-quarter cup Parsons' Ammonia and one quart hot water. Apply with a soft cloth.

■ **Remove mildew from walls.** Scrub with equal parts of Parsons' Ammonia and water.

■ **Clean a crystal chandelier.** Put on cotton gloves, dip your fingers in equal parts Parsons' Ammonia and water, and clean away.

■ **Clean kitchen appliances.** Rub with equal parts Parsons' Ammonia and water.

■ **Remove burned-on grease from glass cookware.** Scrub with equal parts Parsons' Ammonia and water.

■ **Clean golf balls.** Add one-quarter cup Parsons' Ammonia to one cup water, and soak the balls in the mixture.

Invented

4.6 billion years ago

The Name

Parsons' is named after company founder Charles Parsons. The word *ammonia* stems from the Greek word *ammoniakos*, meaning "of Ammon," the Egyptian god, whose temple was near the place where ammonia was prepared.

A Short History

Household ammonia is actually a dilute solution of ammonium hydroxide. Ammonia itself is a colorless, poisonous gas made from hydrogen and nitrogen. The ammonia is then stored either in pressurized cylinders or as an aqueous solution. In the laboratory, ammonia may be prepared by heating an ammonium salt with sodium hydroxide.

Ingredients

Ammonium hydroxide, detergents, fragrance

Strange Facts

■ Ammonia, or NH_3, is one part nitrogen and three parts hydrogen.

■ The electrical energy of lightning causes atmospheric nitrogen and hydrogen to combine to form ammonia. Ammonia combines with rain and becomes available to green plants as dilute nitric acid.

■ Bacteria convert the nitrogen in animal urine into ammonia and atmospheric nitrogen.

■ Fritz Haber and Carl Bosch developed a method for synthesizing ammonia from hydrogen and nitrogen. This Haber-Bosch process is used to manufacture nitrogen fertilizers, ammonia being the principal nitrogen source in fertilizer.

■ Ammonia, although irritating and somewhat toxic, was first used in 1850 as a refrigerant for vapor-compression machines and is still widely used in industrial refrigeration. Ammonia is widely used as a refrigerant because it liquifies easily.

■ Some astronomers believe the Great White Spot on the northern hemisphere of Saturn is an upwelling of ammonia-rich materials that crystallizes to produce the white color.

■ Astronomers theorize that Jupiter has three layers of clouds, the highest being ammonia ice.

■ Astronomer Fred Lawrence Whipple, director of the Smithsonian Astrophysical Observatory, theorizes that comets are composed primarily of frozen ammonia and methane gathered together with dust in a nucleus.

■ Heating stored liquid ammonia to release hydrogen may yield a possible source of energy to power automobiles.

■ Ammonia is the principal ingredient in smelling salts. When inhaled, the fumes irritate the nerve endings in the mucous membranes of the upper respiratory system and the stomach, causing the medulla in the brain to reflex, stimulating breathing and relieving faintness.

■ Greenpeace advises using ammonia to cut through heavy grease and grime, but only as a last resort since fumes irritate eyes and lungs.

■ Never mix ammonia with chlorine bleach or commercial cleansers. Deadly fumes may form.

Distribution

■ Parsons' Ammonia is available in Clear, Sudsy, Lemon, and Pine Scent.

For More Information

Church & Dwight Co., Inc., 469 North Harrison Street, Princeton, NJ 08543-5297. Or telephone 1-800-524-1328. On the Internet, visit www.armhammer.com.

Notes

■ **Avoid parking tickets.** Leave a Post-it Note on the parking meter to let the meter maid know you'll be right back with change for the meter.

■ **Prevent someone from turning off a pre-set VCR.** After setting your VCR to record a show, put a Post-it Note on the control panel so no one turns it off.

■ **Notify others whether dishes in the dishwasher are clean.** Stick a Post-it Note on the front of the dishwasher after turning it on. When the dishwasher stops, the Post-it Note will alert others that the dishes inside are clean.

■ **Remind yourself of necessary chores.** Write important things to do for the next day on Post-it Notes and stick them to the middle of your bathroom mirror.

■ **Remember your destination.** Write down the address of your destination on a Post-it Note and stick it on the inside of the window on the driver's side of the car so you know where you're going.

■ **Learn a foreign language.** Stick Post-it Notes on objects around your house with the word for that object in the language you're trying to learn, like *ventana* (window), *mesa* (table), and *puerta* (door).

■ **Maintain a shopping list.** Keep a running grocery list on a Post-it Note stuck to your refrigerator door.

■ **Be a fashion designer.** Cut out clothing from Post-it Notes for paper dolls.

■ **Play "Pin the tail on the donkey."** Simply write each player's name on a strip cut from a Post-it Note.

■ **Make place cards for a dinner party.** Stick Post-it Notes right on the dinner plates.

■ **Assure telephone messages are received.** Stick a Post-it Note pad near your telephone, so you can post the messages wherever they'll be seen first (on the shower door, television screen, or the telephone receiver itself).

■ **Prevent students from writing in textbooks.** Give students Post-it Notes to stick on pages where they have comments or questions.

■ **Make contracts easy to sign.** Use Post-it Notes to flag where business clients are supposed to sign lines in a contract or application.

■ **Label computer disks temporarily.** After you've filled up the disk, label it permanently.

■ **Remember to take something home from work.** Post a Post-it Note over the light switch in your office so you can't miss it when you turn the light off on your way out the door.

■ **Run a garage sale efficiently.** Post-it Notes make excellent price tags for a garage sale.

■ **Send love notes in your children's lunchboxes.** Stick a Post-it Note inside the cover of your child's lunchbox with a special message.

■ **Prevent leftovers from going bad.** Put Post-it Notes on containers of leftovers in your refrigerator to remind you to eat them by a certain day.

■ **Leave neat graffiti.** Instead of marking up the walls of public restrooms, be a polite graffiti artist by leaving your pithy comment or crude limerick on a Post-it Note.

■ **Protect your eyes and makeup when spraying your hair.** Apply Post-it Notes along your hair line of your forehead.

■ **Don't forget anything before you leave on vacation.** Leave a "to do" list on a Post-it Note posted inside your front door before leaving on a vacation, so you don't forget to turn off all the lights, lock the doors, shut off the gas, check the windows, and bring your airline tickets.

■ **Avoid splattered paint on windows, metalwork, and floors.** Before painting a room, place Post-it Notes along the edge of the glass, over door hinges, and along a linoleum or tile floor where it meets the wall.

Invented
1974

The Name
The Post-it Note gets its name from the fact that this sticky little piece of paper can easily be posted almost anywhere.

A Short History
In 1974, Art Fry, a researcher in product development at 3M, sang each Sunday with his choir at North Presbyterian Church in North St. Paul, Minnesota. He marked the pages of his hymnal with scraps of paper, but the scraps kept falling out, forcing him to constantly scramble to find his place.

"I don't know if it was a dull sermon or divine inspiration," Fry recalled, "but my mind began to wander and suddenly I thought of an adhesive that had been discovered years earlier by another 3M scientist, Dr. Spencer Silver."

While researching ways to develop stronger, high-tack adhesives, Silver had accidentally discovered an adhesive that wasn't very sticky. Convinced that this pseudo-adhesive had untapped potential, Silver had demonstrated his "temporarily permanent" glue to several 3M colleagues, including Fry. At the time, no one had had any idea what to do with it.

Since 3M lets its scientists spend up to 15 percent of their work time on projects of their own choosing, Fry came to work on Monday morning and applied some of Silver's "not-so-sticky" glue to the edge of a piece of paper. One end stuck to the page of his book, the other end stuck out like a bookmark. Fry could also easily reposition the bookmark without damaging the pages. When Fry wrote a note on one of his new bookmarks and attached it to a report he was forwarding to his supervisor, he suddenly realized that his sticky bookmark was actually a new way to pass notes. But 3M company management had no interest in producing a notepad that would sell for a premium price when people could just as easily use ordinary scratch paper.

Fry passed out samples of the sticky little pieces of paper to the secretaries at 3M, figuring they were the people in the company most likely to find uses for them. The secretaries were quickly hooked on Fry's "press-and-peel notes" and soon demanded more. Fry couldn't keep up with the increasing demand, and finally, at the urging of their own secretaries, the top brass gave Fry the green light and a research team. Eighteen months later, Fry and his team showed samples of Post-it Note pads to the 3M marketing department.

In 1977, 3M test-marketed Post-it Notes in four American cities. The results were terrible. Consumers refused to buy a product they had never used before. In desperation, leaders of 3M's Commercial Office Supply Division flew to Richmond, Virginia, and dropped in unannounced at banks and offices to demonstrate the product. By the end of the day, they had stacks of orders. When 3M gave away free samples in Boise, Idaho, nearly 90 percent of the people who tried Post-it Notes said they would buy them. In 1979, 3M launched Post-it Notes on the West Coast of the United States. Demand was so overwhelming, distributors starting shipping Post-it Notes to stores on the East Coast before their full-scale national introduction in 1980.

Ingredients
Paper, adhesive

Strange Facts
■ How do Post-it Notes work? "The adhesives used in Post-it products are made up of tiny globules that make intermittent contact between the Post-it Note and whatever you stick it to," according to the 3M Company. "The resulting bond is storing enough to keep the Post-it Note in place for long periods, but weak enough so that it can be removed or repositioned without harming most delicate surfaces."

■ In the movie *Romy and Michele's High School Reunion*, Romy (Mira Sorvino) and Michele (Lisa Kudrow), plan to impress everyone at their ten-year high-school reunion by telling their classmates that they invented Post-it Notes.

■ In Dick Francis's novel, *Longshot*, the lead character, who is a survival expert and an author, always carries Post-it Notes as a survival tool to make maps, mark a trail, or help start a fire.

■ During a pre-trial hearing in Athens, Georgia, a few defense attorneys were physically separated from the rest of the defense team. To communicate, they stuck Post-it Notes (with possible questions for the witnesses) to an assistant counsel's coat. The assistant would then take the Post-it Notes off his coat and stick them to the chief counsel's legal pad so he could ask the questions.

■ "I like to set out all my serving bowls and platters in advance, then indicate what each will contain on a Post-it that I attach to the rim," Martha Stewart explained on her ninety-second syndicated radio show. "This avoids confusion when pre-dinner activity goes into overdrive. Of course, I always remember to remove them before serving the feast, because while they are a good thing, Post-its don't come in flavors."

■ In a music video by country singer George Jones, the leading lady leaves messages on Post-it Notes scattered throughout the house to communicate with her no-good husband who never listens to her.

■ The *Wall Street Journal* of March 26, 1998, reported: "Yet another use for Post-its was spotted in New York's Grand Central Terminal, where a signboard for the 8:27 P.M. train to North White Plains bore this little yellow note to a commuter: 'Shel—second car.'"

■ In 1996, 3M registered the canary-yellow color of Post-it Notes with the U.S. Patent and Trademark Office, preventing any other company from selling repositionable-note pads printed in canary-yellow.

■ While jeering the abundance of song-and-dance numbers on television shows, a 1997 issue of *TV Guide* complained: "On *Suddenly Susan* and *Fired Up*, for instance, the melodic moments took the form of fantasies and were tacked onto the episodes like scribbled Post-it Notes."

■ In Tom Clancy's bestselling novel *Debt of Honor*, Post-it Notes mark the spots where high-level officials are asked to sign a series of documents.

■ Post-it Note inventor Art Fry has become a cult hero, appearing in ads for the Gap, photographed by Richard Avedon, wearing Gap khaki pants, shoes, and shirt, and his trademark 3M lab coat.

Distribution

■ Post-it Notes are one of the five top-selling office products in the United States.

■ The "not-so-sticky" glue accidentally invented by Spencer Silver is the basis for more than 400 Post-it products (in a wide variety of colors, sizes, shapes, fragrances, and dispensers), ranging from notes to flags, fax labels, and easel pads.

For More Information

3M Consumer Stationery Division, P.O. Box 33594, St. Paul, MN 55133. Or telephone 1-800-364-3577. On the Internet, visit http://www.mmm.com/market/office/postit/.

Pringles

■ **Relieve premenstrual syndrome.**
Eat Pringles before you are about to
have your period. Before menstruat-
ing, women lose a lot of fluid. Potato
chips are high in carbohydrates, which
cause your body to retain fluid and
also give your body more energy.

■ **Revive leather shoes.** Grind
up Pringles with a mortar and
pestle and mix with enough water to make a thick paste. Rub
the mixture into the shoes, wipe
off, then apply polish.

■ **Relieve insect bites.**
Grind up Pringles with a
mortar and pestle and add
enough water to make a
paste. Apply to insect bites
to relieve the itching.

■ **Make black paint.**
Bake Pringles until they're
black. Grind the blackened
Pringles into a fine powder

with a mortar and pestle. Add linseed oil, and mix until you achieve the consistency of paint.

■ **Clean a paint roller.** Fill an empty Pringles can with solvent, put the roller inside, and seal the can with the plastic lid. Shake the can, let sit for two hours, then remove the roller and wash with soapy water.

■ **Store yarn or string.** Run the yarn through a hole punched in the plastic lid of a Pringles can.

■ **Pack paper cups for a picnic.** Five-ounce Dixie Cups fit perfectly inside an empty Pringles can.

■ **Store paintbrushes, colored pencils, or crayons.** Use an empty Pringles can decorated with Con-Tact Paper.

■ **Send cookies through the mail.** Fill an empty Pringles can with home-baked cookies, wrap, and mail.

■ **Store bread crumbs, flours, sugar, pasta, or biscuits.** Cover empty Pringles cans with Con-Tact Paper and label.

■ **Pack jars of baby food for a trip.** An empty Pringles can will hold three jars of Gerber's Baby Food, protected by the paper padding.

Invented
1968

The Name

Pringles seems to be a combination of the words *prince*, meaning "regal," and *shingles*, denoting "chips."

A Short History

In 1968, Procter & Gamble developed stackable potato chips in a vacuum-packed can in order to deliver the chips to grocery stores through the same delivery system used to ship its other products.

Ingredients

Dried potatoes, vegetable oil (containing one or more of the following: corn oil, cottonseed oil, and/or sunflower oil), maltodextrin, wheat starch, salt, dextrose

Strange Facts

■ Pringles Original Flavor contain no artificial ingredients and no preservatives.

■ Procter & Gamble introduced Pringles Potato Crisps at the same time General Foods introduced Pringles Pretzel Snacks. Procter & Gamble ended up buying the rights to the Pringles name from General Foods for an undisclosed sum.

■ Pringles are labeled "Potato Crisps" because the Food and Drug Administration, egged on by genuine-potato-chip manufacturers, ruled that Pringles could be called potato chips only if the words "made from dried potatoes" were printed on the package.

Distribution

■ Pringles are available in Original, Ranch, BBQ, Sour Cream & Onion, Cheezum, Salt & Vinegar, Pizza, Right Crisps, Fat Free, and Ridges.

For More Information

Procter & Gamble, Box 5560, Cincinnati, OH 45202. Or telephone 1-800-568-4035. On the Internet, visit www.pg.com.

Heavy Duty Scrub Sponge

■ **Lure trout.** Coat small pieces of a Scotch-Brite Heavy Duty Scrub Sponge with Vaseline Petroleum Jelly to simulate fish-egg bait.

■ **Remove latex paint from electrical-outlet covers.** Remove the outlet covers from the wall, soak in a sink full of water for one hour, then scrub lightly with a Scotch-Brite Heavy Duty Scrub Sponge.

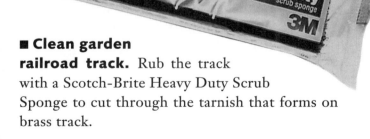

■ **Clean garden railroad track.** Rub the track with a Scotch-Brite Heavy Duty Scrub Sponge to cut through the tarnish that forms on brass track.

■ **Clean tire whitewalls.** Scrub with a damp Scotch-Brite Heavy Duty Scrub Sponge, then rinse with a hose.

■ **Improvise kneepads.** When you're scrubbing the floor or the bathtub, place a Scotch-Brite Heavy Duty Scrub Sponge under each knee. Or sew pockets onto the knees of an old pair of pants and slip sponges inside.

■ **Prevent pots from scratching the sink.** Place a Scotch-Brite Heavy Duty Scrub Sponge under the pot you are about to scour.

■ **Repel raccoons, skunks, squirrels, chipmunks, dogs, and cats.** Soak old Scotch-Brite Heavy Duty Scrub Sponges in a mixture of one part ammonia and one part water and place the sponges where the animals tend to congregate.

■ **Remove lint from furniture or clothing.** Rub with a dampened a Scotch-Brite Heavy Duty Scrub Sponge.

■ **Apply paint.** Cut a Scotch-Brite Heavy Duty Scrub Sponge into any shape you desire, dip in paint, and apply textures to walls and other surfaces.

■ **Remove vinyl decals, graphics, tapes, films, and adhesives without damaging underlying paint.** Simply rub with a Scotch-Brite Heavy Duty Scrub Sponge.

■ **Seal envelopes and adhere stamps.** Cut a Scotch-Brite Heavy Duty Scrub Sponge to fit inside a jar lid, fill with water, and whisk the envelopes and stamps over the sponge.

■ **Improvise a pin cushion.** Push needles and pins into a dry Scotch-Brite Heavy Duty Scrub Sponge.

■ **Soap up excess water from an umbrella stand.**
Place a Scotch-Brite Heavy Duty Scrub Sponge at the bottom of the umbrella stand.

■ **Absorb water and soap scum from a soap dish.** Cut a Scotch-Brite Heavy Duty Scrub Sponge to fit in the base of the soap dish.

Invented
1948

The Name
Scotch-Brite is a combination of the words *Scotch*, meaning "Scottish," and a misspelling of *bright*, describing how your dishes, pots, and pans will look if you use this product.

A Short History
Founded in 1902 by five businessmen, the Minnesota Mining and Manufacturing Company (better known as 3M) originally made sandpaper. In 1925, laboratory employee Richard Drew invented Scotch Brand Masking Tape, followed by Scotch Brand Cellophane Tape in 1929, catapulting 3M to the forefront of innovation, where the company strives to remain, encouraging its scientists to develop products of their own fancy. In 1948, 3M scientists invented non-woven fabrics, leading to the development of Scotch-Brite cleaning and finishing products. In 1959, 3M made Scotch-Brite cleaning pads available to consumers.

Ingredients

Sponge, non-woven abrasive fabric, adhesive, antibacterial

Strange Facts

■ Scotch-Brite Heavy Duty Scrub Sponges are treated with "3M antibacterial technology" to inhibit odor-causing bacteria and mildew-staining in the sponge.

■ Scotch-Brite Heavy Duty Scrub Sponges remove burned-on food better than any other scrub sponge, and last through hundreds of uses.

Distribution

■ 3M makes several dozen Scotch-Brite products.

For More Information

3M Home Care Division, P.O. Box 33068, St. Paul, MN 55133. Or telephone 1-800-363-3577. On the Internet, visit www.3m.com.

Skin-So-Soft

■ Remove makeup. Rub a dab of Skin-So-Soft over your face, then wash clean with water.

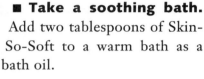

■ Take a soothing bath. Add two tablespoons of Skin-So-Soft to a warm bath as a bath oil.

■ Soften fingernails. Warm Skin-So-Soft and use as a hot oil treatment to soften nails.

■ Enjoy a massage. Skin-So-Soft is an excellent massage oil.

■ Relieve itching from insect bites. Applying Skin-So-Soft to the affected areas alleviates itching.

■ Polish wood surfaces. Squeeze Skin-So-Soft onto a soft cloth to clean and polish natural wood.

■ **Clean grease and dirt.** Squeeze Skin-So-Soft onto a soft cloth to remove grease stains from Formica surfaces and oven-range hoods.

■ **Remove chewing gum from hair or carpeting.** Rub a dollop of Skin-So-Soft into the bubble gum.

■ **Remove dried glue and gum left from price tags and labels from glass, metals, and most plastics.** Apply Skin-So-Soft and wipe clean.

■ **Clean soap scum.** Skin-So-Soft removes soap scum from shower doors, shower curtains, windows, and bathroom and kitchen fixtures.

■ **Remove lime and hard-water deposits from windows, fixtures, shower doors, and tile.** Apply Skin-So-Soft to a cloth and wipe clean.

■ **Remove tar spots from car finishes without damaging the finish.** Apply Skin-So-Soft to a cloth and rub until the tar glides off.

■ **Lubricate pipe joints.** Skin-So-Soft works as an oil lubricant for fitting pipe joints together.

■ **Clean oil-based paint from hands.** Skin-So-Soft removes paint and stains from hands more gently than turpentine does.

■ **Clean ink from hands and vinyl surfaces.** Apply Skin-So-Soft and wipe clean.

- **Get a suntan.** Skin-So-Soft works as a suntan oil.

- **Clean grease and oil from skin.** Rub Skin-So-Soft into the skin and wash clean with water.

- **Clean paintbrushes.** Skin-So-Soft leaves paintbrush bristles feeling soft as new.

- **Remove ring-around-the-collar.** Skin-So-Soft removes the dirt rings in collars when rubbed into the fabric.

- **Remove candle wax.** Rub a dollop of Skin-So-Soft to remove candle wax from furniture, carpeting, and clothing.

- **Remove scuff marks from patent-leather shoes.** Apply Skin-So-Soft to a soft cloth and rub into the patent leather.

- **Pry apart two stacked bowls or glasses.** Dribble a few drops of Skin-So-Soft down the sides, then slip the bowls or glasses apart.

- **Clean vinyl car upholstery.** Apply Skin-So-Soft to a soft cloth and wipe down the seats and other vinyl surfaces.

- **Cleans tape marks left from bandages on skin.** Apply Skin-So-Soft, rub the skin, then wipe clean with a dry cloth.

Invented

1962

The Name

Skin-So-Soft obviously refers to this moisturizer's ability to make skin feel so very soft.

A Short History

During the 1880s, door-to-door book salesman David McConnell gave small bottles of perfume to New York housewives who listened to his sales pitch. Realizing that the perfume was more popular than the books, McConnell created the California Perfume Company in 1886, hiring women to sell door-to-door. Renamed "Avon" in 1950, after the Avon River in England, the company became the world's largest cosmetics company. Avon launched the Skin-So-Soft bath line in 1962.

Ingredients

Purified water, octyl palmitate, glycerine, steareth-20, cetearyl alcohol, steareth-2, glyceryl stearate, xanthan gum, imidazolidinyl urea, methylparaben, triethanolamine, ceteareth-20, carbomer-941, dimethicone, trimethylsil-oxysilicate, fragrance, carbomer-940, disodium EDTA, FD&C blue 1

Strange Facts

■ In the 1960s and 1970s, Avon became a household word thanks to the prevalence of Avon Ladies and television commercials in which a doorbell rings, followed by the catchphrase, "Avon Calling."

■ In 1989, Avon became the first major cosmetics company to end animal testing. Today, Avon actively encourages environmental awareness at all Avon facilities around the world.

Distribution

■ Avon sells its cosmetics, toiletries, and costume-jewelry products through nearly 2.8 million Avon representatives in 135 countries.

■ In 1998, Avon's worldwide sales topped $5.2 billion.

■ The line of Skin-So-Soft products includes Bath Oil, Bath Oil Spray, Moisturizing Bath & Shower Gel, Bath Bar, Antibacterial, Moisture Boast Body Cream, and Mosturizing Dry Oil Body Mist.

For More Information

Avon Products, Consumer Information, 1251 Avenue of the Americas, New York, NY 10020. Or telephone 1-800-367-2866. On the Internet, visit www.avon.com.

■ **Make mulch for your garden.** Shred a copy of *USA Today*, place in your garden bed, and wet down thoroughly.

■ **Dry wet shoes or boots.** Stuff the footwear with crumpled pages from *USA Today*, and let dry overnight (away from a heat source).

■ **Gift-wrap presents.** Use pages of *USA Today* to improvise gift-wrapping paper.

■ **Deodorize luggage.** Fill a suitcase or trunk with crumpled pages of *USA Today*, close, and let sit for two weeks.

■ **Deodorize shoes or boots.** Crumple up pages from *USA Today* and shove into the footwear, let sit overnight. By morning the odors will be gone.

■ **Protect valuables.** When moving, pack boxes with plenty of shredded copies of *USA Today*.

■ **Clean your windows.** Use crumbled-up sheets of *USA Today* to clean glass.

■ **Improvise a dustpan.** It you don't have a dustpan available when sweeping, use a folded-up section of *USA Today*.

■ **Deodorize a plastic food container.** Stuff the container with crumpled pages from *USA Today*, replace the lid securely, and let sit overnight.

■ **Make emergency cat-box litter.** In a pinch, you can uses a shredded copy of *USA Today* in your cat's litter box.

■ **Make recycled paper.** Cut sheets of *USA Today* into long, thin strips (or feed the newspaper through a paper shredder) until you have one-and-a-half cups of packed, shredded newspaper. Put the shredded newspaper into a jar and fill it three-quarters full of hot tap water. Screw on the lid and let stand for three hours, shaking the jar occasionally and beating and stirring with a wooden spoon. As the paper absorbs the water, add more hot water. When the mixture becomes pasty and creamy, pour it into an electric blender. Dissolve three tablespoons of cornstarch in one-half cup of hot water, pour into the blender, and blend. Pour the mixture into a baking pan (larger than 8 by 10 inches). Place a metal screen (8 by 10 inches) on top of the mixture in the baking pan, then gently push it down into the tray until the mixture covers it. Bring the screen up and place it on a sheet of newspaper and press it flat with the palm of your hand to squeeze away the water. Let the screen-backed paper mixture dry in the sun for several hours. When the paper is thoroughly dry, peel it from the screen backing and trim the edges with scissors.

■ **Make starter logs for your fireplace.** Roll up a copy of *USA Today*, secure it tightly with wire, saturate with water from a hose, and let dry. Or tightly roll up a copy of *USA Today* lengthwise, tie in a knot. Several of these will start almost any log on fire.

■ **Clean an oven.** Crumble up sheets of *USA Today* to remove heavy grease from inside an oven, then whip the oven clean with a damp cloth or sponge.

■ **Repel raccoons from cornfields.** When the corn ripens, place crumpled-up pages of *USA Today* between rows of corn.

■ **Improvise a tablecloth.** In a pinch, you can use pages from *USA Today* as a tablecloth.

■ **Avoid painting doors shut.** Fold a page of *USA Today* over the top of the door, close it, then paint.

■ **Stop draft winds from getting into your house.** Roll up several sheets of *USA Today* lengthwise, secure with rubber bands, and with scissors, cut it to the width of your front door. Then squeze the roll of newspaper in the crack under the door to stop drafts from blowing in. You can also stuff newspaper into the cracks around windows.

■ **Ripen green tomatoes before a frost strikes.** Pick the tomatoes, wrap each one in a page of *USA Today*, and let sit for a few days until ripe.

■ **Eliminate cobwebs.** Roll up a section of *USA Today* lengthwise and secure with rubber bands. Using scissors, cut fringes two inches into one end, then use the rolled-up newspaper as duster.

■ **Pad carpeting.** Place a few copies of *USA Today* under rugs and carpets.

■ **Create traction if you get stuck on an icy road.** Place several thicknesses of *USA Today* under the rear wheels to give the tires traction.

■ **Remove a broken windowpane.** Glue a page from *USA Today* to both sides of the windowpane. When the glue dries, chip away the putty, and the pane will come out without shattering.

■ **Repel moths.** Pack wool sweaters in copies of *USA Today*. Moths hate newsprint.

Invented
1982

The Name

USA Today, the first nationally distributed daily newspaper in the United States of America, is named after that fact.

A Short History

In 1982, Allen Neuhart, the chairman of Gannett newspapers, started *USA Today*, the first nationally distributed daily newspaper. In 1993, after losing nearly $600 million, the Gannett daily finally showed a profit.

Ingredients

Newsprint, ink

Strange Facts

■ *USA Today* is nicknamed "McPaper."

■ In 1989, retired *USA Today* founder Al Neuharth, peeved that "young, attractive" flight attendants had been replaced by "aging women" or "flighty young men," demanded the return of "sky girls." According to *Time* magazine, "Employees in the paper's newsroom protested, and Susan Bianchi-Sand, head of the flight attendants' union, wondered if he might be living up to the title of his upcoming autobiography, *Confessions of an S.O.B.*

■ In 1990, Cincinnati Bengals coach Sam Wyche banned *USA Today* football reporter Denise Tom from the Bengals' locker room after the team lost to the Seattle Seahawks. "I will not allow women to walk in on fifty naked men," insisted Wyche. After *USA Today* sent a letter of protest to the National Football League demanding that the league enforce its 1985 policy of equal access to players for male and female journalists, the NFL fined Wyche one-seventeenth of his annual salary—an estimated $30,000, the highest penalty ever levied against an NFL coach.

■ When *USA Today* founder Al Neuharth retired in 1989 at the age of sixty-five, Gannett gave him stock worth $5.1 million and $300,000 a year, guaranteed for life.

Distribution

■ *USA Today* is the bestselling daily newspaper in the United States.

For More Information

USA Today, 1000 Wilson Blvd, Arlington, VA 22229. Or telephone 1-703-276-3400. On the Internet, www.usatoday.com.

Wish-Bone

Thousand Island Dressing

■ **Remove a ring stuck on a finger.** Smear on some Wish-Bone Thousand Island Dressing and slide the ring off.

■ **Remove white rings and spots from wood furniture.** Wipe on Wish-Bone Thousand Island Dressing, let stand for an hour, and wipe off.

■ **Polish wood furniture.** Squeeze Wish-Bone Thousand Island Dressing onto a soft cloth to clean and polish natural wood.

■ **Remove candle wax from wood or Formica furniture.** Rub a dollop of Wish-Bone Thousand Island Dressing to remove candle wax from wood or Formica.

■ **Remove dried glue and gum left from price tags.**
Apply Wish-Bone Thousand Island Dressing and wipe clean.

■ **Remove tar.** Spread a teaspoon of Wish-Bone Thousand
Island Dressing on tar, rub, and wipe off.

■ **Pry apart two bowls or glasses.** Dribble a few drops
of Wish-Bone Thousand Island Dressing down the sides,
then slip the bowls or glasses apart.

Invented
1957

The Name
Wish-Bone is named after the Wish-Bone Restaurant, which was
named after the V-shaped clavicle bone of a chicken or turkey.

A Short History
In 1945, the Wish-Bone Restaurant opened in Kansas City,
Missouri, specializing in chicken and serving salad dressing
made from a recipe brought by the owner's mother from her
native country, Italy. When patrons began asking for samples
of the salad dressing for use at home, the owner bottled and
sold the dressing in the restaurant. The owner eventually
sold the restaurant and went into the salad dressing business,
selling four varieties: Italian, Russian, French, and Cheese.
In 1957, Lipton purchased the business, added new varieties
(including Thousand Island), and marketed Wish-Bone Salad
Dressings nationwide.

Ingredients

Soybean oil, high-fructose corn syrup, water, sour pickle relish (cucumber, distilled vinegar, salt, turmeric), distilled vinegar, tomato paste, salt, contains less than 2 percent of egg yolk (dehydrated), spice, natural flavors, onion (dehydrated), algin derivative, xanthan gum, calcium disodium EDTA (to preserve freshness)

Strange Fact

■ The custom in which two people each make a wish—and tug on opposite ends of a wishbone until one breaks off the larger piece—originated with the Etruscans as early as 400 B.C.E.

■ The Wish-Bone Salad Dressing bottle is designed in the shape of a wishbone.

Distribution

■ Wish-Bone salad dressings are available in Italian, Robusto Italian, Creamy Italian, Ranch, Chunky Blue Cheese, Classic Caesar, Creamy Caesar, Deluxe French, Sweet 'n Spicy French, Honey Dijon, Oriental, Red Wine Vinaigrette, White Wine Vinaigrette, Balsamic Vinaigrette, Olive Oil Vinaigrette, Roasted Garlic Vinaigrette, Sun Dried Tomato Vinaigrette, Berry Vinaigrette, and Thousand Island.

For More Information

Lipton, 800 Sylvan Avenue, Englewood Cliffs, NJ 07632. Or telephone 1-800-697-7887. On the Internet, visit www.wish-bone.com.

And Much, Much More

Accent® Flavor Enhancer

■ **Prevent coprophagy.** Accent Flavor Enhancer is monosodium glutamate, a digestive enzyme that can be used by pet owners to prevent a pet from eating its own feces. Adding one teaspoon of Accent Flavor Enhancer to the pet's food twice daily for three days should put an end to the nasty habit. **For more information:** The Pillsbury Company, 2866 Pillsbury Center, Minneapolis, MN 55402-1464. Or telephone 1-800-767-4466. On the Internet, visit www.pillsbury.com.

Ocean Spray® Cranberry Juice Cocktail

■ **Treat urinary-tract infections.** Drink Ocean Spray Cranberry Juice Cocktail every day. A Harvard University study, published in the March 9, 1994, issue of the *Journal of the American Medical Association*, found that regular consumption of Cranberry Juice Cocktail may help maintain urinary-tract health. **For more information:** Ocean Spray Cranberries, Inc., Lakeville Middle-boro, MA 02349. Or telephone 1-800-662-3263. On the Internet, visit www.oceanspray.com.

Scope® Cool Peppermint

■ **Keep flies off horses.** Mix equal parts Scope Cool Peppermint Mouthwash with Baby Oil in a sixteen-ounce trigger spray bottle, and spray on your horses. **For More Information (on Scope's oral care use):** Procter & Gamble, Cincinnati, OH 45202. Or telephone 1-800-543-7270. On the Internet, visit www.pg.com.

Speed Stick®

■ **Freshen the air in your home.** Apply a Speed Stick to an incandescent lightbulb and then turn on the lamp. The heat from the lightbulb will slowly melt the deodorant, freshening the air in the room. **Hide valuables.** Unscrew the deodorant stick completely, place valuables inside the plastic canister, replace the deodorant stick, and cap. **For more information:** The Mennen Co., Morristown, NJ 07962-7408. Or telephone 1-800-228-7408. On the Internet, visit www.mennen.com.

For more offbeat uses for brand-name products,
visit Joey Green on the Internet at
www.wackyuses.com

Acknowledgments

My editor, Richard F.X. O'Connor, courageously fought for my right to continue sharing hundreds of offbeat uses for brand-name products with the American public. I am grateful for his passion, keen wit, and very warm heart.

I am also indebted to Jeremy Solomon, Bill Hartley, Michael Teitelbaum, Kimbria Hays, and an army of copyeditors and proofreaders.

In the corporate world, I am deeply indebted to Karen Woros and Elena Neus at Nabisco Foods (makers of A.1. Steak Sauce), Wendy Salustro at Playtex Products, Inc. (makers of Baby Magic Baby Powder), John Norris, Jr., and Rhonda Paris at Dairy Association Co, Inc. (makers of Bag Balm), Suzanne Mears at Campbell Soup Company (makers of Campbell's Tomato Soup), Greg Zimpritch and Leslie Himley at General Mills, Inc. (makers of Cheerios), Sharon Ptak-Miles and Becky Haglund-Tousey at Kraft Foods, Inc. (makers of Cheez Whiz, Cool Whip, and Country Time Lemonade), Robert H. Black and Leela Damm at Automation, Inc. (makers of Clean Shower), Jim Bogie and Diane Manwaring at MedTech (makers of Cutex Nail Polish Remover), John McLaughlin and Julien Hecht at DAP, Inc. (makers of DAP caulk), Suzy Carroll, Jill Burress, Doris Lucas, and Kim Yee, at Dr Pepper/Seven-Up Companies (makers of Dr Pepper), Milly Walker at the Dr Pepper Museum, Sandy Sullivan at the Clorox Company (makers of Formula 409), Tom Knuessel at Diamond Brands (makers of

Forster Clothes Pins), Barbara Yaros at Reckitt & Colman, Inc. (makers of French's Mustard), Amanda Hamilton at Bender-Hammelering Group, Andy Horrow at the Gatorade Company (makers of Gatorade Thirst Quencher), Fred Haymond and Chuck Sinclair at Goodyear (makers of Goodyear Tires), Scott Thompson at Colgate Palmolive (makers of Irish Spring Soap and Mennen Speed Stick), Karin Chiappetta at Favorite Brands International (makers of Jet-Puffed Marshmallows), Bob Weir at Eastman-Kodak (makers of Kodak Film), Bertille Glass and Marlene Machut at M&M Mars (makers of M&M's Chocolate Candies), Brad Norman at Luther Ford & Company (makers of Mrs. Stewart's Liquid Bluing), Mary Jon Dunham and Mary Blair at Procter & Gamble (makers of Noxzema, Pringles, and Scope Cool Peppermint), Judy Schuster at 3M (makers of Post-it Notes and Scotch-Brite Heavy Duty Scrub Sponges), Debbie Coffey at Avon Products (makers of Skin-So-Soft), Barbara Maxwell and Lisa Leevy-Washington at *USA Today*, Ann Arnold Debur and Rowena DeLeon at Lipton, Inc. (makers of Wish-Bone Thousand Island Dressing), Gerard Meyer at B&G Foods (makers of Accent Flavor Enhancer), and Cindy Taccini at Ocean Spray Cranberries, Inc. (makers of Ocean Spray Cranberry Juice Cocktail).

Above all, all my love to Debbie, Ashley, and Julia.

The Fine Print

Sources

■ *All-New Hints from Heloise* by Heloise (New York: Perigee, 1989)

■ *Another Use For* by Vicki Lansky (Deephaven, MN: Book Peddlers, 1991)

■ *Ask Anne & Nan* by Anne Adams and Nancy Walker (Brattleboro, VT: Whetstone, 1989).

■ *Can You Trust a Tomato in January?* by Vince Staten (New York: Simon & Schuster, 1993)

■ *A Dash of Mustard* by Katy Holder and Jane Newdick (London: Chartwell Books, 1995).

■ *Dictionary of Trade Name Origins* by Adrian Room (London: Routledge & Kegan Paul, 1982)

■ *The Doctors Book of Home Remedies* by Editors of Prevention Magazine (Emmaus, PA: Rodale Press, 1990)

■ *The Doctors Book of Home Remedies II* by Sid Kirchheimer and the Editors of Prevention Magazine (Emmaus, PA: Rodale Press, 1993)

■ *Encyclopedia of Pop Culture* by Jane & Michael Stern (New York: HarperCollins, 1992)

■ *Famous American Trademarks* by Arnold B. Barach (Washington, D.C.: Public Affairs Press, 1971).

■ *Hints from Heloise* by Heloise (New York: Arbor House, 1980)

■ *Hoover's Company Profile Database* (Austin, TX: The Reference Press, 1996).

■ *Hoover's Guide to Private Companies 1994-1995* (Austin, TX: The Reference Press, 1995).

■ *Household Hints & Formulas* by Erik Bruun (New York: Black Dog and Leventhal, 1994)

■ *Household Hints for Upstairs, Downstairs, and All Around the House* by Carol Reese (New York: Henry Holt and Company, 1982)

■ *Household Hints & Handy Tips* by Reader's Digest (Pleasantville, NY: Reader's Digest Association, 1988)

■ *How the Cadillac Got Its Fins* by Jack Mingo (New York: HarperCollins, 1994)

■ *Kitchen Medicines* by Ben Charles Harris (Barre, MA: Barre, 1968)

■ *Make It Yourself* by Dolores Riccio and Joan Bingham (Radnor, PA: Chilton, 1978)

■ *Mary Ellen's Best of Helpful Hints* by Mary Ellen Pinkham (New York: Warner/B. Lansky, 1979)

■ *Mary Ellen's Greatest Hints* by Mary Ellen Pinkham (New York: Fawcett Crest, 1990)

■ *Our Story So Far* (St. Paul, MN: 3M, 1977)

■ *Panati's Extraordinary Origins of Everyday Things* by Charles Panati (New York: HarperCollins, 1987)

■ *Practical Problem Solver* by Reader's Digest (Pleasantville, NY: Reader's Digest, 1991)

■ *Rodale's Book of Hints, Tips & Everyday Wisdom* by Carol Hupping, Cheryl Winters Tetreau, and Roger B. Yepsen, Jr. (Emmaus, PA: Rodale Press, 1985).

■ *Symbols of America* by Hal Morgan (New York: Viking, 1986)

■ *Why Did They Name It . . . ?* by Hannah Campbell (New York: Fleet, 1964)

■ *The Woman's Day Help Book* by Geraldine Rhoads and Edna Paradis (New York: Viking, 1988)

Trademark Information

"A.1." is a registered trademark of Nabisco Brands Company. Nabisco, Inc., does not recommend, endorse, or accept any liability for any uses for A.1. Steak Sauce other than its intended use for food. The A.1. name and photograph of A.1. bottle are used with permission.

"Baby Magic" is a registered trademark of the Mennen Co.

"Bag Balm" is a registered trademark of Dairy Association Co, Inc. The Dairy Association Co, Inc., does not endorse, recommend, or accept liability for any suggested use of Bag Balm other than those uses indicated on the package label.

"Campbell's," "M'm! M'm! Good!," "Pepperidge Farm," "Franco-American," "V8," "Swanson," and "Godiva" are registered trademarks of Campbell Soup Company and used with permission. Campbell Soup Company does not endorse or recommend any use of Campbell's tomato soup beyond those for which the product has been tested as indicated on the usage instructions on each label or in product promotional material distributed by or on behalf of the company.

"Cheerios" is a registered trademark of General Mills, Inc.

"Cheez Whiz," "Cool Whip," and "Country Time" are registered trademarks of Kraft Foods, Inc. Kraft Foods, Inc., does not endorse any use of Cheez Whiz, Cool Whip, or Country Time Lemonade other than the intended uses of the products as indicated on their packaging labels.

"Clean Shower" is a registered trademark of Clean Shower, L.P.

"Cutex" is a registered trademark of MedTech, Inc.

"DAP" is a registered trademark of DAP, Inc. DAP, Inc., does not endorse, recommend, or accept liability for any mentioned use of Dynaflex 230 Sealant that is not specifically endorsed in the product's packaging and labeling.

"Dr Pepper," "Dr," and "Pepper" are registered trademarks of Dr Pepper/Seven-Up, Inc.

"Forster" is a registered trademark of Diamond Brands, Inc.

"French's," "Frank's," and "RedHot" are registered trademarks of Reckitt & Colman, Inc. Reckitt & Colman does not recommend, endorse, or accept liability for any use of French's Mustard other than as a food condiment.

"Gatorade" is a registered trademark of the Gatorade Company. Neither the Gatorade Company nor the Quaker Oats Company accept any liability for any use of Gatorade other than as a beverage.

"Goodyear" is a registered trademark of Goodyear, Inc.

"Irish Spring" is a registered trademark of Colgate-Palmolive. Colgate-Palmolive Company does not recommend or endorse any use of Irish Spring Soap other than those uses indicated on the package label.

"Jet-Puffed" is a registered trademark of Favorite Brands International, Inc.

"Kodak" and "Max" are registered trademarks of Eastman Kodak Company.

"M&M's" is a registered trademark of M&M Mars, Co.

"Mrs. Stewart's" is a registered trademark of Luther Ford & Company. Luther Ford & Company does not endorse any uses for Mrs. Stewart's Bluing other than those indicated on the package label or in current company brochures.

"Noxzema," "Pringles," "Potato Crisps," and "Scope" are registered trademarks of Procter & Gamble. Procter & Gamble does not recommend, endorse, or accept liability for any use of Noxzema, Pringles, or Scope beyond those uses for which the products have been tested as indicated on the usage instructions on each package label. Photographs used with permission.

"Parsons'" is a registered trademark of Church & Dwight Company. Church & Dwight Co., Inc. does not recommend uses of Parsons' Ammonia not described on the product label or in current company brochures.

"Post-it" and "Scotch-Brite" are registered trademarks of 3M.

"Skin-So-Soft" is a registered trademark of Avon Products.

"USA Today" is a registered trademark of Gannett News Service.

"Wish-Bone" is a registered trademark of Lipton, Inc.

"Accent Flavor Enhancer" is a registered trademark of B&G Foods.

"Ocean Spray" is a registered trademark of Ocean Spray Cranberries, Inc.

"Speed Stick" is a registered trademark of the Mennen Co.

Photograph on page 181 copyright © 2000 by Debbie Green. All rights reserved. Used with permission.

Index

Biscuits, storing
Pringles, 136
Blood
Clean Shower, 32
Boat buffer pads
Goodyear Tires, 82
Boating, storing money
Kodak Film, 98
Bolts, rusty
Dr Pepper, 55
Parsons' Ammonia, 123
Boots
deodorizing, *USA Today*, 148
drying, *USA Today*, 148
sorting, Forster Clothes Pins, 67
Bottles
cleaning, Parsons' Ammonia, 123
deodorizing, French's Mustard, 71
Bowling pins
Gatorade, 78
Bowls, prying apart
Noxzema, 116
Skin-So-Soft, 145
Wish-Bone, 155
Brass
A.1. Steak Sauce, 1
Campbell's, 13
Formula 409, 61
Parsons' Ammonia, 123
Bread crumbs, storing
Pringles, 136
Breast inflamation
Castor oil, 19
Bridge tables
Campbell's, 13
Bumper guards
Goodyear Tires, 82
Bumper stickers, removing
Cutex, 49

Burns
Cool Whip, 40
Bursitis
castor oil, 20

Cabinet doors
DAP Caulk, 52
Camping
Irish Spring, 87
Kodak Film, 97, 98
Candle holder
Campbell's, 14
Candle wax
Skin-So-Soft, 145
Wish-Bone, 154
Candles, making
Campbell's, 14
Carpet
cleaning, Parsons' Ammonia, 121
padding, *USA Today*, 151
spots, Formula 409, 61
stains, Clean Shower, 34
Cat box litter
USA Today, 149
Cats
injuries, Bag Balm, 10; Scotch-
Brite, 140
urine stains, Parsons' Ammonia, 121
Cattle injuies
Bag Balm, 10
Chandelier, cleaning
Parsons' Ammonia, 124
Cheerios Treats
Cheerios, 24
Cheez Whiz burgers
Cheez Whiz, 29
Cheez Whiz dip
Cheez Whiz, 30

Mustard dressing
French's Mustard, 72

Nails and screws
Campbell's, 14
Cool Whip, 41
Irish Spring, 88
Kodak Film, 97
Necklaces, detangling
Baby Magic, 6
Nipples, sore
Bag Balm, 9
Nose, sore
Bag Balm, 10

Oil and grease stains
Parsons' Ammonia, 121
Organizing
boots, Forster Clothes Pins, 67
cables, Forster Clothes Pins, 65
desk drawers, Kodak Film, 98
papers, Forster Clothes Pins, 68
Oven, cleaning
Clean Shower, 34
Parsons' Ammonia, 120
USA Today, 150
Oven-range hoods
Skin-So-Soft, 144

Paint
cleaning, Cutex, 48; Noxzema,
115; Scotch-Brite, 140;
Skin-So-Soft, 145
electrical-outlet plates,
Scotch-Brite, 139
making, Pringles, 135
odor, Parsons' Ammonia, 122

storing, Cool Whip, 41
Paint roller, cleaning
Pringles, 136
Paintbrushes
cleaning, Skin-So-Soft, 145
making, Forster Clothes
Pins, 67
storing, Pringles, 136
Painting
doors, *USA Today*, 150
splatters, Post-it Notes, 129
Paper clips
Forster Clothes Pins, 68
Paper cups, packing
Pringles, 136
Paper dolls
Post-it Notes, 128
Parking tickets, avoiding
Post-it Notes, 127
Pasta, storing
Pringles, 136
Pet food, storing
Gatorade, 77
Pets, whitening
Mrs. Stewart's, 107
Picnics
paper cups, Pringles, 136
table clothes, Forster Clothes
Pins, 67
Pills
Kodak Film, 97
Pin cushions
Scotch-Brite, 141
Pin the Tail on the Donkey
Post-it Notes, 128
Pipe joints, lubricating
Noxzema, 115
Skin-So-Soft, 145
Place cards
Post-it Notes, 128

Saddle sores
Bag Balm, 9
Salt and pepper
Kodak Film, 97
Sand
Baby Magic, 6
Sandals
Goodyear Tires, 82
Sapphires
Parsons' Ammonia, 120
Saw blade, lubricating
Irish Spring, 88
Scissors
Cutex, 49
Scuff marks
Cutex, 47
Noxzema, 115
Skin-So-Soft, 145
Sculpting
Mrs. Stewart's, 109
Sewing
hemming, Forster Clothes Pins, 66
kit, Kodak Film, 97
pin cushion, Irish Spring, 88
Shaving
Baby Magic, 6
Cheez Whiz, 30
Cool Whip, 40
Noxzema, 116
Sheets
cleaning, Parsons' Ammonia, 122
sticky, Baby Magic, 6
Shirts
Baby Magic, 6
Shoes
deodorizing, Irish Spring, 87;
USA Today, 148
drying, *USA Today*, 148
repairing, DAP Caulk, 52

patent leather, castor oil, 19
polishing, A.1. Steak Sauce, 1;
Baby Magic, 6; Cool Whip, 39;
Formula 409, 61
reviving, Pringles, 135
scuff marks, Cutex, 47; Noxzema,
115; Skin-So-Soft, 145
softening, castor oil, 21
Shopping
Forster Clothes Pins, 66
Post-it Notes, 128
Shower doors
Skin-So-Soft, 144
Silver, cleaning
Cool Whip, 40
Parsons' Ammonia, 122
Sinks
cleaning, Clean Shower, 32, 33
protecting, Scotch-Brite, 140
Skid pads
Goodyear Tires, 82
Skin, soothing rough
Noxzema, 116
Skunks
odor, Campbell's, 12
repelling, Scotch-Brite, 140
S'mores
Jet-Puffed Marshmallows, 93
Sneakers
cleaning, Baby Magic, 6;
Cutex, 47
deodorizing, Irish Spring, 87
repairing, DAP Caulk, 52
Soap dish
Scotch-Brite, 141
Soap scum
Skin-So-Soft, 144
Soldering
Forster Clothes Pins, 65

About the Author

Joey Green, author of *Polish Your Furniture with Panty Hose, Paint Your House with Powdered Milk*, and *Wash Your Hair with Whipped Cream*, got Jay Leno to shave with Jif peanut butter on the *Tonight Show*, had Katie Couric drop her diamond engagement ring in a glass of Efferdent on *Today*, and has been seen polishing furniture with SPAM on *CNN Headline News* and cleaning a toilet with Coca-Cola in the *New York Times*. A former contributing editor to *National Lampoon* and a former advertising copywriter at J. Walter Thompson, Green is the author of ten books, including *Joey Green's Encyclopedia of Off-*

*   Prod-
                iritual
            nbow*, and *The Bubble Wrap*
            Florida, and a graduate of Cornell
        vision commercials for Burger King
        and won a Clio Award for a print ad
        Kodak. He backpacked around the
        his honeymoon, and lives in Los
        Debbie, and their two daughters,

Ashley and Julia.